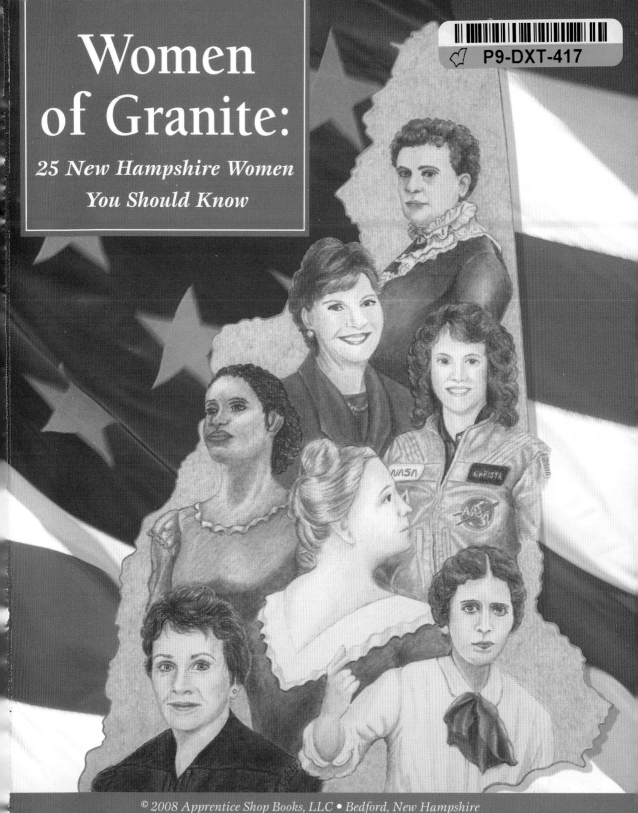

Women of Granite:

25 New Hampshire Women You Should Know

P9-DXT-417

© 2008 Apprentice Shop Books, LLC • Bedford, New Hampshire

Written by Janet Buell and The Write Sisters • Illustrated by Lisa Greenleaf

Apprentice Shop Books, LLC
Bedford, New Hampshire

For information regarding permissions contact:
Apprentice Shop Books, LLC
7 Colby Court, Box 156
Bedford, NH 03110
www.apprenticeshopbooks.com

LIBRARY OF CONGRESS CATALOGING-IN-PUBLICATION DATA

Buell, Janet.
Women of Granite: 25 New Hampshire Women You Should Know by Janet Buell and the Write Sisters. Illustrations copyright © 2008 by Lisa Greenleaf
Summary: Profiles of 25 influential New Hampshire women. Includes bibliographies for additional research.

1. New Hampshire, Juvenile non-fiction. 2. Famous New Hampshire women. 3. Women artists—United States—New Hampshire—biography—juvenile literature. 4. Women athletes—United States—New Hampshire—biography—juvenile literature. 5. Women writers—United States—New Hampshire—biography—juvenile literature. 6. Women in public service—United States—New Hampshire—juvenile literature.

ISBN 9 7809723410-4-8

Oceanic Graphic Printing, Inc.
105 Main Street
Hackensack, NJ 07601

Printed in China

On the cover: Clockwise from bottom left: Senior Associate Supreme Court Justice Linda Stewart Dalianis; Author Harriet Wilson; former New Hampshire Governor Jeanne Shaheen; Attorney/activist Marilla Ricker; Teacher/astronaut Christa McAuliffe; Labor activist Elizabeth Gurley Flynn; Soprano and activist Caroline Gardner Bartlett.

Cover design, illustrations and book design by Lisa Greenleaf
www.Lisagreenleaf.com

A Note from Jeanne Shaheen

My family and I moved to New Hampshire in 1973. Since that time, I've come to love its scenery, its Yankee spirit, and its traditions.

What I find most charming about New Hampshire are its people. Whether they were born in the Granite State or have adopted it as their own, the character of the landscape shines through its citizens. I'm proud to live among people who are known for an independence of mind and spirit.

Women of Granite has introduced me to 24 exceptional women who represent New Hampshire's spirited and strong-minded outlook. Even though they come from different times and backgrounds, they show us what we already know. Women can accomplish anything they put their minds to.

I'm honored to be included in a book with so many notable New Hampshire women. I hope, like me, you will be inspired by their stories.

Jeanne Shaheen

Author/Writer Credits

"Amias Thompson: Settler," "Lucy Howe Crawford: Innkeeper," and "Harriet E. Adams Wilson: African American Novelist" copyright © 2008 by Sally Wilkins

"Ona (Oney) Maria Judge Staines: A Thirst for Freedom," "Betsey Chamberlain: A Chance to Write," "Mary Bradish Titcomb: She Worked Hard at Her Craft," and "Elizabeth Gurley Flynn: Fighting Injustice" copyright © 2008 by Diane Mayr

"Mattie Knight: Distinguished Bag Lady," "Bernice Blake Perry: NH's Queen of the Air," "May Gruber: Knitting the Pandora Empire," and "Jeanne Shaheen: NH's First Elected Woman Governor" copyright © 2008 by Janet Buell

"Marilla Ricker: Suffragette," "Doris Ethel 'Granny D' Rollins Haddock: Fighting for a Better America," "Penny Pitou: She Keeps Going and Going and..." "Marian MacDowell: An Ordinary Woman" copyright © 2008 by Barbara Turner

"Caroline Gardner Bartlett: Nurse or Spy?" "Persis Foster Eames Albee: Business Pioneer," "Elizabeth Orton Jones: Old Girl, You are an Artist!" copyright © 2008 by Andrea Murphy

"Lotte Jacobi: Photographic Artist," "Elizabeth Yates: Newbery Award Winning Author," "Linda Stewart Dalianis: NH's First woman Supreme Court Justice," and "Lynn Jennings: Distance Runner," copyright © 2008 by M. Lu Major

"Annalee Thorndike: Doll Maker and Businesswoman," "Christa McAuliffe: Teacher in Space," and "Jenny Thompson: Olympic Swimmer" copyright © 2008 by Kathleen W. Deady.

Photo and Illustration Credits

Cover—background photo from Veer.

Pages 7, 12, 22, 32, 37, 47, 57, 72: illustrations by Lisa Greenleaf.

Page 15, in the public domain.

Pages 17 and 19 by permission of the Dartmouth College Libraries Special Collections.

Page 24, in the public domain.

Page 27, photo by Lisa Greenleaf.

Page 29, photos of bottles courtesy of Donald V. Fadely author of *Hair Raising Stories*.

Page 34, patent of Mattie Knight's bag folding machine, in the public domain.

Page 42, courtesy of the MacDowell Colony.

Page 44, courtesy of the United States Post Office.

Page 49, courtesy of the Woodrow Wilson House Museum, Washington, DC.

Pages 52 and 54, photos of Caroline Bartlett in the public domain.

Page 59, doll courtesy of Andrea Murphy; photo by Lisa Greenleaf.

Page 62 and 64, photos courtesy of the Library of Congress.

Pages 67 and 69, photos courtesy of the Lotte Jacobi Collection, University of New Hampshire Media Services.

Page 74, photo courtesy of David Gaudes.

Page 77, photo courtesy of Muriel L. Dubois.

Page 82, photo courtesy of the Special Collections and University Archives, University of Oregon Libraries.

Page 84, photos from Pickety Place, courtesy of Muriel L. Dubois.

Page 87, photo of Granny D. courtesy of Douglas Prince.

Pages 92 and 94, photos courtesy of May Gruber.

Page 97, photo courtesy of Concord Monitor, Concord, NH.

Page 99, dolls courtesy of Aimée Dubois; photo by Lisa Greenleaf.

Pages 102 and 104, photos courtesy of Penny Pitou.

Page 107, 109, and 119, photos courtesy of Associated Press.

Page 112 and 114, photos courtesy of NASA.

Page 117, photo by George Peet, courtesy of the New Hampshire State Supreme Court.

Page 122, photo by Mike Powell, courtesy of Getty Images.

Page 124, photo by Gray Mortimer, courtesy of Getty Images.

Page 127, photo by Adam Pretty, courtesy of Getty Images.

Page 129, photo by Donald Miralle, courtesy of Getty Images.

Table of Contents

— 1 —
Amias Thompson:
Settler

by Sally Wilkins

$\mathcal{A}$mias Thompson stood by the table, listening. Miles Standish was telling her husband, David, about the trouble at the Plimoth, Massachusetts colony. Three ships had arrived bringing more **Puritan** families. For three years the Plimoth settlers had struggled. In England they had been town dwellers, not farmers. Now, there were more mouths to feed and not enough food. Could the Thompsons help?

Amias did not pity the Puritans. She had grown up in town, too. She had been a shopkeeper, selling herbs and ointments in an **apothecary** shop. The Thompsons had been in New Hampshire for only four months. They had built a sturdy log house and Amias had planted a garden as soon

TIDBITS

One of Amias' first visitors was completely naked. Thomas Weston, had been cast ashore by a storm and then had all his clothing stolen by local Indians.

as they arrived. As a result, the meal she served Captain Standish included fish and a few early vegetables.

Standish kept talking. The Plimoth settlers were hungry. They also feared the Indians might attack.

The Thompsons agreed to do what they could. David packed a boat with fish and followed Standish back to Plimoth. He would be gone at least a week. Amias would manage. She always managed.

· · · · ૭૭ · · · ·

Amias Cole was born in 1595 in Plymouth, England. Her father was a shipbuilder. She was just 17 when she married David Thompson. David was a Scotsman. He was interested in the exploration of the New World.

David and Amias Thompson crossed the Atlantic in 1623 on the *Jonathan*. The Thompson's four-year old son, John, and seven workmen were also on board. Amias left her daughter Pricilla with her parents. The Thompsons settled on what is now Odiorne Point in the Piscataqua River. They called the settlement Pannaway.

The Pannaway settlers set **weirs** in the river to catch fish. They dried the fish in the sun. While the settlers at Plimoth were building barricades against the Indians, the Thompsons planted gardens. They traded plants and furs with the Abenaki and Penacook.

When Miles Standish visited, Amias was the only European woman in New Hampshire. Later, the Hilton family moved to New Hampshire. They settled at Dover Point. But their home was seven miles up the river from Pannaway. Amias could not drop in at Mary Hilton's for a cup of tea!

In 1626, David was appointed Acting Governor of the whole New England region. David and Amias moved to Noddles Island near Boston. Pannaway was abandoned. David died just two years later. At age 35, Amias married their neighbor, Samuel Maverick. She and Samuel had four children.

When **smallpox** struck, Amias's skills as an apothecary were important to the settlers. But Amias also went to the Indian village to nurse the sick. She and Samuel took Wampanoag orphans home to care for them.

Years later, Samuel was appointed a Royal Commissioner, settling disputes among colonists. The Duke of York gave him a house lot on Manhattan. While Samuel traveled, Amias moved to Maine with her daughter, Mary. Amias lived to be at least 80 years old.

TIDBITS

Amias and David Thompson's first neighbors, the Hiltons, left the Plimoth colony because the Puritans refused to baptize their baby.

◆

Noddles Island is now part of Boston's Logan Airport.

Timeline: Amias Thompson

1595 ▸ Amias Cole is born to William and Agnes Cole of Plymouth, England.

1613 ▸ Marries David Thompson, a Scotsman.

1615 ▸ A daughter, Ann, is born at the end of September, dies October 14.

Amias and David open an apothecary shop in Plymouth.

1616 ▸ Daughter Pricilla is born.

1619 ▸ Son John is born.

David travels to New England with an exploration party, a year before the *Mayflower* **Pilgrims** settle there in Plimoth, Massachusetts.

1620 ▸ Daughter (also named Ann) is born, dies in less than a week.

1622 ▸ David Thompson receives a 6000 acre grant from The New England Company. David settles in New Hampshire to protect the company's fishing rights and establish trade with the Indians.

1623 ▸ January, the Thompsons sail from England for New Hampshire. Pricilla Thompson (age 7) is left in England with her grandparents.

March, The Thompsons settle at Odiorne Point.

July, Miles Standish arrives from the Plimoth colony to ask for food.

1626 ▸ David Thompson is asked to oversee both the Massachusetts and New Hampshire colonies. The Thompsons move to Noddles Island in Boston Harbor.

1627 or 28 ▸ David Thompson dies.

1630 ▸ Amias marries Samuel Maverick.

1633 ▸ December, a smallpox outbreak kills most of the people in Winnisimmet Massachusetts. Amias nurses the sick Indians and brings Indian orphans back to her house to care for them.

1635–1666 ▸ Samuel travels a great deal on business. In the 1660s Amias moves to Saco, Maine to live with her daughter, Mary.

c1675 ▸ Amias dies. No exact date of her death is listed.

NOTE: c1675 means about or around 1675.

Learn More about the Earliest Settlements of New England

- Bowen, Gary. *Stranded at Plimoth Plantation 1626.* (HarperCollins, 1994).
- Deady, Kathleen W. *The New Hampshire Colony.* (Fact Finders: American Colonies) Capstone Press, 2006.
- Hakim, Joy. *A History of US, Book 2: Making Thirteen Colonies.* (Oxford University Press, 2002).
- Maestro, Betsy and Giulio. *The New Americans: Colonial Times: 1620-1689.* (HarperTrophy, 2004).

Websites:

- Colonial New Hampshire:
  http:www.usahistory.info/New-England/New-Hampshire.html
- A Brief History of New Hampshire:
  http://www.nh.gov/nhinfo/history.html

Glossary

apothecary (uh PAWTH i ker ee) Also called chemist. Apothecaries collected, preserved, compounded, and sold plant and animal substances used for treating wounds and illnesses.

Pilgrim (PIL gruhm) Pilgrims were people traveling for a religious purpose. The *Mayflower* settlers did not use the term Pilgrim to describe themselves; later historians did.

Puritan (PYOOR uh tuhn) The Puritans were a religious movement in England who wanted to "purify" or reform the Anglican church. They were known for very strict, plain living. The Massachusetts Bay Colony was governed by Puritans until 1685.

smallpox (SMAWL poks) A highly contagious illness that killed more than 30 % of its victims. The virus came to the New World with the settlers, triggering massive epidemics among the Native Americans, who had no immunity to the germ.

weir (wihr) A system of nets on racks in a river designed to capture and hold fish.

— 2 —
Ona (Oney) Maria Judge Staines:
A Thirst for Freedom

by Diane Mayr

*G*eorge Washington wanted his slave back. He sent Burwell Bassett to do the job.

In the three years since her escape, Oney had married. She had given birth to a daughter, Eliza. When a child was born to a slave the baby also, became the **property** of the slave owner. Oney would not let her child be a slave.

Bassett found Oney in Portsmouth, New Hampshire. He told her to go back to the Washingtons. She would be forgiven for running away.

Forgiven? Oney did not want forgiveness. She wanted her freedom! She told Bassett, "I am free now and choose to remain so."

Bassett made plans to take Oney and her child by force. Oney found out about the plan. Quickly she dressed the baby. She gathered their things. Oney hired a carriage and late at night they left Portsmouth. For a second time she escaped.

· · · · ◠◡ · · · ·

Ona Maria Judge was born in Virginia around 1773. Her mother, Betty, was one of Martha Washington's slaves.

Her father was a tailor, Andrew Judge. Andrew was a white **indentured** servant. Oney, as she was called, had light skin and many freckles.

When she was around ten years old, Oney moved into the Washingtons' home.

George Washington wrote, "she was handy and useful." She also learned to sew.

Washington was elected president. Oney now did more than sew. She helped Martha Washington to dress and do her hair.

The Washingtons moved to Philadelphia, Pennsylvania in 1790. Oney went, too.

Pennsylvania was not a slave state. Slaves who lived in Pennsylvania could be granted their freedom after six months. Washington made sure that his wife's slaves were not set free. He sent them back and forth to Mount Vernon.

Mrs. Washington was getting old. When she died, her property would be given to her grandchildren. Oney was Mrs. Washington's property.

Oney wanted to be free. In 1796 she made plans to escape. "I had friends among the colored people of Philadelphia, had my things carried there beforehand, and left Washington's house while they were eating dinner." Oney boarded a ship and traveled to New Hampshire. When she landed, Oney thought she was free.

One day, she heard someone call her name. Elizabeth Langdon had been a visitor at the Washington home. She recognized Oney and tried to talk with her. Oney hurried away. The Langdons

TIDBITS

In the south light-skinned slaves generally became "house slaves," while dark-skinned slaves worked in the fields.

New Hampshire's Constitution, adopted in 1784, states "All men are born equally free and independent." It did not give freedom to New Hampshire's slaves, but anyone who was born after 1783 couldn't be enslaved in New Hampshire.

TIDBITS

In the first U.S. **census** of 1790, 158 slaves are listed for New Hampshire. By the 1830 census, there were 5.

•◆•

An 1845 article in the *Granite Freeman* stated, "She came on board a ship commanded by Capt. John Bolles, and bound to Portsmouth, Later, she added, 'I never told his name till after he died. . . lest they should punish him for bringing me away.'"

told the Washingtons that Oney was in Portsmouth.

The Washingtons were angry. They wanted Oney to return. The President asked businessman Joseph Whipple for help. Washington said that Oney had been taken away by a Frenchman. Whipple spoke with Oney and found that she had left on her own. She had, "a thirst for complete freedom," Whipple wrote to Washington. Whipple would not send Oney back. He feared dock workers would riot if he tried.

In January of 1797, Oney Judge married John Staines, a free black sailor. The couple lived in Portsmouth where they had a daughter, Eliza.

John often was away at sea. He was gone in the fall of 1799 when Washington sent Burwell Bassett to Portsmouth. Oney refused to return to Washington. She and Eliza hid with friends, John and Phyllis Jack.

George Washington died in 1799. Little is known about Oney Judge Staines after this time. She had another daughter, Nancy, around 1802. She may have had a third child. Oney's husband and children died before she did.

Oney ended up living with the Jack family in Greenland, New Hampshire. The Jacks were free blacks, but very poor. After a difficult life, Oney passed away on February 25, 1848.

Three years before she died, she was interviewed. She said that after Washington's death, "they never troubled me any more…" But Ona Maria Judge Staines was never really free. Martha Washington's family could have forced Oney to return. It was the law.

Timeline: Ona Maria Judge Staines

c1773 ► Born at Mount Vernon, Virginia, exact date unknown. She is a slave to Martha Washington.

c1783 ► Joins the Washington household.

1789 ► George Washington becomes the first President of the United States. Oney travels to New York as Martha Washington's personal slave.

1790 ► Moves to Philadelphia with the President and his wife.

1793 ► Washington signs the **Fugitive** Slave Act. The law forces free states to return fugitive slaves to their owners in slave states.

1796 ► Escapes from the Washingtons in Philadelphia. She travels on the ship, *Nancy,* to Portsmouth, New Hampshire. Washington asks Joseph Whipple to arrange for her return. Oney refuses to go back.

1797 ► Marries John Staines, a free black sailor. She gives birth to a daughter, Eliza, later in the year, or early 1798.

1799 ► Washington sends Burwell Bassett to arrange for Oney's return. Oney escapes capture. December 14, George Washington dies.

c1802 ► Gives birth to daughter, Nancy.

1848 ► Dies on February 25, 1848, in Greenland, New Hampshire. She is buried in an unknown grave.

NOTE: c1773 means about or around 1773.

Washington's Home in Mount Vernon

Learn More about Ona Marie Judge Staines and Her Times

- Giblin, James Cross. *George Washington: A Picture Book Biography*. Scholastic, 1992.

- Kamma, Anne. *If You Lived When There Was Slavery in America*. Scholastic, 2004.

- McCully, Emily Arnold. *The Escape of Oney Judge: Martha Washington's Slave Finds Freedom*. Farrar, Straus and Giroux, 2007.

- Sirimarco, Elizabeth. *The Time of Slavery*. Benchmark Books, 2006.

Websites:

- Slavery at the President's House:
  http://www.ushistory.org/presidentshouse

Glossary

census (SEN suhss) An official count of all the people living in a certain area.

fugitive (FYOO juh tiv) Someone who is running from the law. A slave who escaped was fugitive. If captured, the fugitive would be punished and returned to the slave-owner.

indentured (in DEN churd) Being bound by a contract to work for another for a specific number of years.

property (PROP ur tee) Anything that is owned by a person.

Lucy Howe Crawford:
Pioneer and Innkeeper

by Sally Wilkins

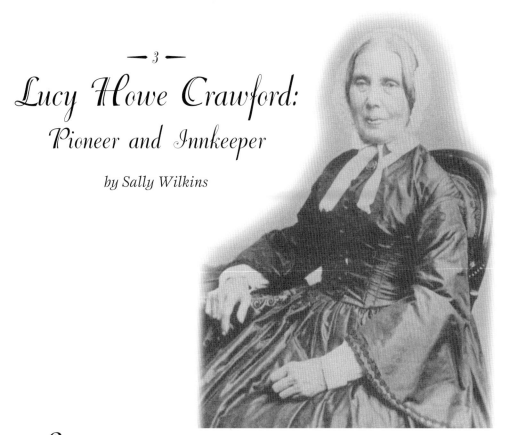

*L*ucy Crawford packed apples, bread and dried meat into Ethan's rucksack and checked the cider in his jug. She wished she could join him on the climb. How she longed to see the view from Mount Washington! This week his hiking party included three sisters. The Austins would be the first women to reach the summit of the highest peak in the East.

Lucy knew she couldn't be away from the inn for four days. She had a nursing baby and two other little ones. And could her hired girls run Moosehorn Lodge?

· · · · ⌒ · · · ·

Lucy Howe was born in 1793 in Guildhall, Vermont. Her grandparents, Eleazar and Hannah Rosebrook, had been among the very first settlers in what is now Colebrook, New Hampshire.

TIDBITS

Lucy and Ethan kept tame deer, bears and other animals so their guests could see the wildlife of the White Mountains.

—•—

Lucy called Ethan "the Giant of the Mountains." He sometimes carried an exhausted hiker on his shoulder.

In 1816 Eleazar developed cancer. Hannah asked Lucy to come be his nurse. A grandson, Ethan Crawford, came to manage the New Hampshire farm. When Eleazar died, Lucy and Ethan married and stayed with Hannah.

To earn money Ethan and the hired men worked building roads. The day Lucy's first child was born, while Ethan was bringing lunch to the road crew, the house caught fire. Lucy and her grandmother rescued as many of the family's possessions as they could. Lucy stuffed all their important papers into a bag. She carried full dresser drawers outside. She was trying to save the clock when Grandmother said they had done all they could. She took the newborn baby and ran into the yard. There was no way to save the house, or the pig in the pen at the back. When Ethan returned only a shed and a barn were still standing. Almost all the food they had was destroyed. A traveling **tinsmith** emptied his cart and gave the exhausted family a ride to the nearest neighbor's house.

Ethan and Lucy began rebuilding right away. A few weeks later, some visitors stopped at the unfinished house. They were looking for a place to stay and a mountain guide.

Mountain climbing was a new sport in the 1820s. People came from the cities seeking fresh air and adventure. So Lucy and Ethan created a resort. Ethan built trails and **bridle paths** and led hikes. Lucy supervised the help, planned meals, and assisted guests. In the evenings the Crawfords entertained visitors with stories and games.

In winter **teamsters** hauling goods through the mountains to and from Vermont stayed at Moosehorn Lodge. Every summer more tourists arrived. Lucy said the house was so crowded the **featherbeds** would touch, but the sheets were clean.

In 1825, Lucy finally did climb Mount Washington. She said the view was too beautiful to describe.

Trouble was never far away. In 1826 floods ruined their farm. The Crawfords borrowed to rebuild again, but they never made enough money to pay back the loans. In the 1840s Ethan became very sick. To raise money, Lucy wrote a book about their lives together. But **creditors** took the inn.

After Ethan died, Lucy moved to Lowell, Massachusetts. Two of her daughters ran boarding houses there for mill girls, using skills they learned at the inn. As her children married, Lucy moved from one home to another, wherever, she said, she could be most useful. When she died in 1869, she was buried with Ethan near the mountain passage now called Crawford **Notch**.

The Crawford's Inn: Moosehorn Lodge

Timeline: Lucy Howe Crawford

1793 ▸ September 5, Lucy Howe is born to Samuel and Mercy (Rosebrook) Howe of Guildhall, Vermont.

1817 ▸ May 4, Lucy moves into her grandparents' New Hampshire home in Fabyan's Purchase to nurse her grandfather, Eleazar Rosebrook.

1817 ▸ September, Grandfather Rosebrook dies. Lucy and Ethan marry November 1.

1818 ▸ July 18, First child, a son Harvey is born prematurely. Later that day a forgotten candle starts a fire in the kitchen. The house is completely destroyed.

1821 ▸ August 31, Eliza, Harriet, and Abigail Austin of Portsmouth climb Mount Washington.

1825 ▸ August, Lucy climbs to the summit of Mount Washington.

1826 ▸ Torrential rains wash out roads and flood the Crawford farm. Animals drown, fields are covered with gravel, and buildings damaged or destroyed.

1833 ▸ Lucy is too ill feed her new baby. A family whose newborn had died adopts the baby.

1835 ▸ Last (tenth) child, William, born.

1836 ▸ Ethan jailed for failing to pay debts.

1837 ▸ Ethan and Lucy give up the inn and move to Vermont. Lucy begins to write a book based on her journals and their memories.

1843 ▸ Family moves back to the Notch, to a rented house across the street from the lodge.

1846 ▸ June 22, Ethan dies. First edition of Lucy's *History of the White Mountains* published.

1847 ▸ Lucy and remaining children join older daughters in Lowell boarding houses.

1853 ▸ Moosehorn Lodge (renamed White Mountain House) destroyed by arson.

1860 ▸ Living with her daughter in Lancaster, Lucy finishes an expanded edition of her book.

1869 ▸ February 16, Lucy dies. She is buried in a family cemetery near where US Route 302 passes through Crawford Notch.

Learn More about Early Tourism in the White Mountains

- Blos, Joan. *A Gathering of Days: A New England Girl's Journal, 1830-32.* Aladdin, 1990.
- Boardman, Julie. *When Women and Mountains Meet.* Durand Press, 1991.
- Cross, George N. *Dolly Copp and the Pioneers of the Glen 1927.* Jackson Historical Society reprint 2003.
- Hawthorne, Nathaniel. "The Notch of the White Mountains" and "Our Evening Party among the Mountains" in *Sketches from Memory or Twice told Tales.* (numerous editions).

Websites:

- American Antiquarian Society on Summer Vacationing in New England: http://www.americanantiquarian.org Type in "mountain resorts" in the search area.
- New Hampshire Historical Society on Grand Hotels: http://www.nhhistory.org/popresorts.html
- Crawford Notch State Park: http://www.nhstateparks.com/crawford.html
- Mount Washington State Park: http://www.nhstateparks.com/washington.html

Glossary

creditor (KRED it ur) A person who loans money to another.

bridle path (BREYE duhl path) A track or path for riding or walking horses.

featherbed (FETH ur bed) A thin mattress made of cloth and stuffed with feathers.

notch (NOCH) A narrow opening between mountains.

teamster (TEEM stur) A person with a team of horses or oxen who transported goods over land for pay.

tinsmith (TIN smith) A craftsperson who made and repaired lightweight metal ware such as pots, pans, and lamps.

— 4 —
Betsey Chamberlain:
A Chance to Write

by Diane Mayr

*B*etsey Chamberlain had come to Lowell, Massachusetts to work in the **mills**. She knew she would have to work hard, but Betsey had always worked hard. Moving to Lowell was both frightening and exciting. Frightening because Betsey was from a small country town and Lowell was a city. Exciting because in Lowell women could attend classes, lectures, and plays. In Lowell there were lending libraries and bookstores. There was even a **journal**, *The Lowell Offering*, which published mill girls' writings. Betsey loved the idea of learning. And, she had a chance to become a published writer!

· · · · ∾ · · · ·

On December 29, 1797 Betsey Guppy was born in a little town near Wolfeboro, New Hampshire. Her father, William Guppy and her mother, Comfort Meserve, were farmers. It is believed that Betsey's grandmother was an Abenaki Indian. It is also believed that because of their mixed race blood, the family often faced **discrimination**.

When Betsey was four years old, her mother died. Two years later, her father remarried. Betsey wrote of her stepmother, "the spirit of kindness dwelt in her." Although her family life was unsettled, Betsey seemed to enjoy her childhood. She remembered how she "played whirl-the-plate, blind-man's-buff, and hurly-burly." She liked school and even worked as a teacher for a short time.

Betsey married Josiah Chamberlain in 1820. They had two children. Josiah died in 1823. Betsey was left alone to raise her two babies. She had to sell off the Chamberlain's home and land. Life became a struggle.

By 1830, Betsey Chamberlain, and her sister, Harriet Guppy, moved to Newmarket, New Hampshire. They found work in the mills. The following year, they went to Lowell, Massachusetts. For a while Betsey and her family moved between the mills in Newmarket and Lowell. They eventually settled in Lowell. Betsey worked in the mills or in **boarding houses**.

Betsey wrote for *The Lowell Offering* and *The New England Offering*. Her work was published under several names. She used Tabitha, Jemima, Betsey, and her initials, B.C. Her writing told of her childhood. In her stories the town called "Salmagundi"

TIDBITS

There are no known pictures of Betsey, only this written description: "She had inherited Indian blood, and was proud of it. She had long, straight black hair, and walked very erect. .."

Betsey Chamberlain was one of the first Native American writers to be published.

Mill workers were called "operatives" during Betsey's time.

TIDBITS

Betsey's son, became a news-paper writer for the New York Herald. His son, Samuel Selwyn Chamberlain, was a news-paperman, too. He became one of the "fathers of **yellow journalism**." Samuel's son (Betsey's great grandson), W.H. Chamberlain, worked for the New York Evening World newspaper. Writing ran in the family!

was really her hometown of Wolfeboro.

Betsey also wrote pieces that spoke up for the Native people who were being treated unkindly. Betsey wanted equality for all. One of her articles was titled, "A New Society." In it she wrote of a place where girls would be educated as well as boys. Where people would work eight hours a day instead of ten or more. Where women would be paid the same as men. Betsey knew it was only a dream, but it did not stop her from writing about it.

Betsey moved to Illinois in 1843 when she married Charles Boutwell. There they started a farm. A few years later she went back to Lowell, perhaps to make some extra money.

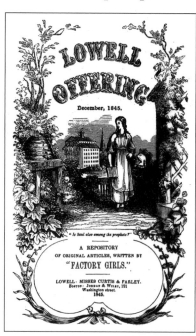

Finally, though, Betsey returned to Illinois to stay. After her husband died in 1863, she lost part of the farm. She lived out the rest of her life with her daughter, Comfort. On September 24, 1886, Betsey Chamberlain died at the age of 88 years. It's possible that she published other writing, but none has been found.

Betsey wrote for the Lowell Offering

Timeline: Betsey Chamberlain

1797 ➤ December 29, born in Brookfield, New Hampshire.

1798 ➤ The family moves to Wolfeboro.

1802 ➤ Betsey's mother dies.

1803 ➤ Her father remarries.

1820 ➤ June 25, marries Josiah Chamberlain.

1820–1823 ➤ Gives birth to Ivory, a son, and Comfort, a daughter.

1823 ➤ Husband Josiah dies.

1830–1839 ➤ Moves between the mills of Newmarket, New Hampshire and Lowell, Massachusetts where she eventually settles.

1834 ➤ Marries Thomas Wright. It is not known when or why the marriage ended.

1840 ➤ Publishes her first work in *The Lowell Offering*.

1843 ➤ Marries Charles Boutwell in Illinois. Settles on a farm in Wayne Township, IL.

1848 ➤ Returns to Lowell. Publishes in *The New England Offering*.

1850 ➤ Permanently returns to Illinois.

1863 ➤ Charles Boutwell dies.

1866 ➤ Marries A. I. Horn. This marriage, too, ended for reasons unknown.

1886 ➤ September 24, dies in Wayne Station, Illinois.

Learn More about Betsey Chamberlain and the Mills of Lowell, Massachusetts

- Flanagan, Alice K. *The Lowell Mill Girls*. ("We the People" series.) Coughlan, 2005.
- Isaacs, Sally Senzell. *Life in a New England Mill Town*. ("Picture the Past" series.) Heinemann, 2002.
- McCully, Emily Arnold. *The Bobbin Girl*. Dial, 1996.
- Newell, William Wells. *Games and Songs of American Children*. Dover, 1963.

Websites:

- Ne-Do-Ba: Friends- Sharing in History. "Betsey (Guppy) Chamberlain:" www.avcnet.org/ne-do-ba/bio_gup1.html
- The Native people of the Northeast. "Abenaki Culture and History Menu" www.avcnet.org/ne-do-ba/menu_his.shtml

Glossary

boarding houses (BORD ing HOUSS ez) Living quarters supplied by a company for its workers.

discrimination (diss KRIM uh NAY shuhn) Treating people unfairly or with prejudice.

journal (JUR nuhl) A magazine or newspaper.

mills (MILLZ) Large factories with machinery for processing textiles, wood, paper, steel, etc.

yellow journalism (YEL oh JUR nuhl iz ihm) A form of newspaper writing that exaggerates or misreports stories to attract readers.

Harriet E. Adams Wilson:
African-American Novelist

by Sally Wilkins

HARRIET E WILSON

Hattie Adams closed her eyes and put her fingers in her ears. She didn't want to hear Mr. Hayward and his mother shouting. She didn't want to believe her own mother was never coming back.

Mr. Hayward's mother wanted to send Hattie to the **poorhouse**. Mr. Hayward wanted to give Hattie a home. He knew his mother would not let Hattie stay out of kindness. He tried to convince her to keep Hattie as her slave.

Only he didn't say "slave." He used a short, mean word. Hattie had heard people say it to her father, who was black. She had heard people spit it at her mother, who was white. People who used that word usually treated black people like farm animals. Now the Haywards were using it for Hattie. She thought she should run away, but where could a five-year-old go?

· · · · ❧ · · · ·

TIDBITS

Slavery became illegal in New Hampshire in 1783. It did not, however, free those who were already slaves.

•◆•

Frederick Douglass and other abolitionists spoke at a rally in Milford in January 1843 when Hattie was 18.

•◆•

Scholars have not figured out why Harriet used the last name "Adams."

Harriet Adams was born in Milford, New Hampshire on March 25, 1825. Hattie's alcoholic mother left her at the Hayward home in 1830. Hattie became their **indentured servant**. For twelve years she did dishes and laundry, sewed clothes and fetched firewood and herded cows.

Some of the family members were kind to Hattie. They sent her to school with the other children. Hattie loved to read. She propped a book open to read while she worked. But Mrs. Hayward beat Hattie. She made her work even when she was sick.

When Hattie turned eighteen, she left the Haywards. Another family was glad to hire her. But years of abuse had made Hattie sick and lame. She could not do housework anymore. Hattie moved to Massachusetts to work as a **seamstress**. She learned to stitch straw bonnets. She discussed books and went to anti-slavery rallies with friends.

One day Harriet met Thomas Wilson, a **fugitive** slave who spoke at rallies. Harriet and Thomas married and settled in Milford. Harriet was happy. Soon she would have a child of her own. But Thomas Wilson was a fake. He was not an escaped slave, and he was not ready to care for a wife and child. Thomas disappeared. In 1852, Harriet's son George was born at the county **poor farm.** Later she would learn Thomas had died in New Orleans.

In 1852 Harriet Beecher Stowe published the anti-slavery novel *Uncle Tom's Cabin*. Many copies of the book were sold. Some people became **abolitionists** after reading it. Harriet Wilson decided she would write a book, too. She wanted to earn money to support herself and her son. She wanted readers to know that even in the north some people treated blacks as slaves. She hoped if a black woman wrote a book, people would see she was not an animal.

Harriet wrote a novel about a little girl whose life was very much like her own. The hateful word from her past became the title of Harriet's book. *Our Nig* was published in Boston in 1859, just before the Civil War. Hattie hoped it would earn a better future for her son. But George caught fever and died the next year. He was just seven.

Scholars are still learning more about Harriet's life. After the Civil war she move to Boston. She made and sold Mrs. H.E. Wilson's Hair Regenerator. Newspapers advertised "Dr. Harriet Wilson," a popular **spiritualist** speaker. She died in 1900, a very accomplished old woman.

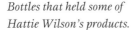

Bottles that held some of Hattie Wilson's products.

TIDBITS

Milford was an important stop on the Underground Railroad.

•◆•

Harriet E. Wilson was the first African-American to have a novel published in the United States.

•◆•

Harriet's book was rediscovered and republished in 1983.

•◆•

Cruel Mrs. Hayward was a cousin of the Hutchinson Singers, who were famous abolitionists.

Timeline: Harriet E. Adams Wilson

1825 ➤ March 15, Harriet E. Adams is born in Milford, NH to Margaret Smith and Joshua Green.

c1828 ➤ Joshua Green dies of consumption (tuberculosis).

1830–31 ➤ Unable to support her, Harriet's mother leaves her at the Nehemiah Hayward family farm.

1832–1838 ➤ Harriet attends Milford District School No. 3 for three months each year.

1843 ➤ January, Frederick Douglass speaks at an anti-slavery rally in Milford. March, Her indenture over, Harriet moves to the Boyles home in Milford.

1850 ➤ Harriet begins work in W (probably Worcester), Massachusetts.

1851 ➤ October 6, Harriet E. Adams marries Thomas Wilson.

c1852 ➤ Thomas leaves for a lecture tour and does not return when expected. Spring - Harriet is taken to the County Poor Farm in Goffstown. June 15, Her son, George Mason Wilson is born in early summer.

1859 ➤ September 5, Harriet's novel *Our Nig* is published in Boston.

1860 ➤ February 16, Wilson's son George dies.

1863 ➤ Harriet Wilson's name appears on the Report of the Overseers of the Poor for the town of Milford.

1867 to 1897 ➤ "Dr." Harriet Wilson is a popular Spiritualist speaker in Boston.

1870 ➤ Harriet travels to Chicago as a delegate to the American Spiritualist Society Convention. September 29, Harriet E. Wilson of Milford, N.H. marries John Gallatin Robinson in Boston.

1900 ➤ June 28, "Hattie E. Wilson" dies in Quincy, Massachusetts where she was buried.

NOTE: c1828 means about or around 1828.

Learn More about Harriet Wilson and the Abolitionist Movement

- Carson, Mary Kay. *The Underground Railroad for Kids: From Slavery to Freedom with 21 Activities (For Kids Series)*. Chicago Review Press, 2005.

- Devereaux, Anne Jordan and Schomp, Virginia. *Slavery And Resistance (The Drama of African American History)*. Benchmark Books, 2006.

- McNeese, Tim *The Rise and Fall of American Slavery: Freedom Denied, Freedom Gained (Slavery in American History)*. Enslow Publishers, 2004.

Websites:

- Center for New England Culture resources on Harriet Wilson:
  http://neculture.org/harriet_wilson.html

- Harriet Wilson Project:
  http://www.harrietwilsonproject.org

- National Park Service information on Opposition to Slavery:
  http://www.nps.gov/ugrr/TEMPLATE/FrontEnd/learn_a3.cfm

Glossary

abolitionist (AB uh LISH uh nist) Abolitionists opposed slavery and worked to have it abolished (ended) in the United States.

fugitive (FYOO juh tiv) Someone who is running from the law. A slave who escaped was fugitive. If captured the fugitive would be punished and returned to the slave-owner.

indentured servant (in DEN churd SUR vuhnt) A free-born person who was sold into slavery for specific number of years.

poorhouse or poor farm (POOR houss or POOR farm) A home owned by a town or county where homeless people could live and raise food.

seamstress (SEEM struhss) A woman who made clothes for other people. Most sewing was done by hand.

spiritualist (SPIHR uh CHOO uh list) Spiritualists believed the living could be helped by the spirits of the dead.

Margaret (Mattie) Knight:
Distinguished Bag Lady

by Janet Buell

Margaret Knight sat in the courtroom and listened to **witnesses**. At the other table sat Charles Annan. Margaret claimed Annan had stolen her invention idea. The trial would decide whose invention it really was.

Margaret had come to win. It would cost her almost $2000 for two weeks of trial. That was big money for 1870, but Margaret had a lot at stake. Margaret had invented a machine that cut, folded, and glued square-bottomed paper bags. In the late 1800s, everyone used flimsy, envelope-bottomed bags.

Margaret worked for the Columbia Paper Bag Company. On the job, she studied the bag-making machines. She thought about how a machine could make a better bag – a flat-bottomed bag. She wrote and drew and tinkered. She tested thousands of paper bags on the machines she created. Finally, Margaret came up with a working wooden model of her new machine.

At a machine shop, Margaret's wooden prototype was being made into an iron model. Charles Annan was a visitor to the shop. He recognized just how important Margaret's invention was. He copied the plans. Within weeks, he'd **registered** a **patent** for it at the U.S. Patent office. If she couldn't stop him, Charles Annan would be known as the machine's inventor.

Margaret thought Charles Annan was no better than a common thief. Worse yet, he stated in court that Margaret couldn't have invented the bag-making machine. He claimed only a man was smart enough to understand complicated machinery.

· · · · ೧೦ · · · ·

Margaret Knight was born in 1838. She was plenty smart. Inventive, too. When she was a kid, she built sleds and kites for her brothers. The boys loved their creative sister, whom they called Mattie.

Life wasn't always kind to the Knight family. When Mattie was nine years old, her father died. The family moved to Manchester, New Hampshire. Mattie's mother and brothers found work in the Amoskeag Mills. Mattie brought their lunches to them as they worked -- long, thirteen hour days. Soon Mattie was working in the mills, too.

One day, she was standing near a worker when a weaving **shuttle** flew off the machine into the operator's head. Flying shuttles weren't a new problem for mill workers. Plenty of men had tried to invent a way to keep this from happening. No one succeeded.

TIDBITS

Square-bottomed bags are known as S.O.S. This stands for as "stand-on-shelf" or "self-opening sacks". Today, in excess of 7,000 machines worldwide produce flat-bottom paper bags.

Workmen reportedly refused Margaret's advice when first installing the equipment. They didn't think Margaret knew anything about machinery.

Mattie was a natural-born thinker. She had her father's tools and had learned to use them. Mattie thought up an invention that stopped shuttles from flying into people. Mill owners and workers loved it. In time, weaving machines all over the world included Mattie's invention.

She never made a dime from that invention. That didn't matter. She was happy to help. It didn't stop her from inventing. During her 76 years of life, Mattie developed about ninety inventions. She received patents for 22 of them. Among Mattie's inventions were a silent automobile motor, rotary engines, a window and sash, shoe manufacturing equipment, and improvements to the can-making machine.

Back in the courtroom, Mattie showed the judge her notebooks. They were filled with drawings, notes, and her thoughts about square-bottomed bags. The judge declared that Mattie had invented the machine. Charles Annan had not. She was granted a patent for it in 1871. New Hampshire's Lady Edison proved that women are as smart—and inventive – as men.

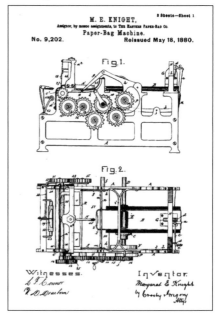

This machine is one of the more than six dozen inventions by American-born inventor Margaret Knight.

Timeline: Margaret (Mattie) Knight

1838	►	February 14, Mattie is born in York, Maine to James Knight and Hannah Teal.
1847	►	Mattie gets her first job as a mill worker in Manchester, NH. She's nine years old, and will work in mills until she is 56 years old.
1850	►	At twelve years old, Mattie invents a stop action **device** for loom shuttles.
1868	►	Mattie goes to work at the Columbia Paper Bag company where she starts working on an invention for a square-bottomed bag.
1870	►	Margaret founds the Eastern Paper Bag Company in Hartford, Connecticut. She launches her court battle against Charles Annan.
1871	►	Margaret Knight wins her court battle against Charles Annan. July 11, Margaret Knight's bag machine is patented. Its patent number is #116,842.
1871–1879	►	Margaret makes and patents other inventions that improve her bag-making machine. She continues making other inventions after that, too.
1914	►	October 12, Margaret dies at 76 years old. She is credited with about 89 inventions and at least 22 patents in her lifetime.
2006	►	Margaret Knight is inducted into the National Inventors Hall of Fame for her Improvement in the Paper-Bag Machine – Patent No. 220,925.

Learn More about Margaret Knight and Her Times

- Blashfield, Jean F. *Women Inventors*. Capstone Press, 1996.
- Brill, Marlene Targ. *Margaret Knight, Girl Inventor*. Millbrook Press, 2001.
- McCully, Emily Arnold. *Marvelous Mattie: How Margaret E. Knight Became an Inventor*. Farrar, Straus and Giroux, 2006.
- Tucker, Tom. *Brainstorm!: The Story of Twenty American Kid Inventors*. Farrar, Straus and Giroux, 1998.

Websites:

- General invention website:
  http://www.invent.org/
- Photo of Mattie's bag-making machine:
  http://www.smithsonianlegacies.si.edu/objectdescription.cfm?ID = 92

Glossary

device: (di VISSE) A piece of equipment that does a particular job.

patent: (PAT uhnt) A legal document giving the inventor of some item sole rights to manufacture or sell the item.

registered: (REJ uh sturd) To enter something into an official site.

shuttle: (SHUHT uhl) The part of the loom that carries the thread from side to side.

witnesses: (WIT niss uhz) People who have seen or heard something.

— 7 —
Marilla Ricker:
Suffragette

by Barbara Turner

Marilla walked into the Dover Town Hall. Friends and neighbors–all men–were gathered there. Marilla said hello, then picked up a **ballot**. As she filled it in, the men stared. Some of them whispered.

Marilla finished filling in her ballot and presented it to the town selectmen. The selectmen stared at her, then at each other. What was she trying to do? Women weren't allowed to vote!

They sent Marilla packing!

Marilla left. She had expected to be turned away, but she did not give up. She knew it was the trying that counted, and for the rest of her life, Marilla kept trying to vote.

· · · · ᘎ · · · ·

TIDBITS

At age 16, Marilla began teaching in New Durham, New Hampshire. She did not believe in the Bible or God. When the school committee insisted she have her students read from the Bible, Marilla turned to the story of Jonah being swallowed by the whale. She said, "We will now read the startling and truthful account of Jonah whilst he was a sojourner in the sub-marine hotel."

Marilla Young was born in New Durham, NH on March 18, 1840. Her mother was religious. Her father was not. He believed people should reason things out and use common sense. Marilla grew up believing what her father believed. As a child, she refused to go to church or say her prayers. Instead, she helped her father on their farm, and went with him to political meetings.

At age 23, Marilla married John Ricker, a farmer and businessman. John was 33 years older than Marilla. They moved to Dover, NH, and five years later, John died.

Marilla was suddenly wealthy. She could do as she pleased. In 1869 she attended the first meeting of the National Women's Suffragette Association. **Suffragettes** were women who fought for women's rights. It was after returning from this meeting that Marilla first tried to vote. She realized that asking men to grant women equal rights would never work. Women would only gain their rights by doing the work themselves.

> "I have found that men will listen to all your arguments readily and then will go home and forget everything you have said."

In 1876, Marilla went to Washington, DC to study law. Six years later she passed the **bar exam**. She returned to New Hampshire to practice law there, but the state would not allow it. That didn't stop Marilla. She sued the state for the right to practice law and won the case.

Marilla had opened a door for women, but it was only one door, and there were many more to open. She returned to Washington, and became a member of the US Supreme Court

Bar. She became involved in politics. In 1897, she applied to become **Ambassador** to the South American country of Columbia. This position was usually given to someone from New Hampshire. Once more, she was turned down because she was a woman. Marilla wasn't discouraged. Trying was what mattered, and in 1910, she tried again. She would run for Governor of New Hampshire.

> "I'm running for Governor in order to get people in the habit of thinking of women as Governors . . . People have to think about a thing for several centuries before they can get acclimated to the idea. I want to start the ball rolling."

Marilla wasn't allowed to run. Only voters could run for office, and women still weren't allowed to vote. But Marilla did get the ball rolling, and in 1996, Jeanne Shaheen was elected the first woman Governor of New Hampshire. Because of Marilla and women like her, it did not take several centuries.

In August, 1920, women finally gained the right to vote. Three months later, at the age of eighty, Marilla Ricker died. No one knows if she ever cast her vote.

TIDBITS

As a lawyer, Marilla worked most often with the poor. It is said she never once charged anyone for her legal services. She always worked for free.

•◆•

Marilla said, "Nothing grows slower than truth, and nothing faster than superstition."

Timeline: Marilla Ricker

1840	►	Marilla Marks Young is born in New Durham, NH on March 18.
1855	►	Enters Colby Academy for 1 year of teacher training.
1856	►	Begins teaching in New Durham, NH district schools.
1861	►	Civil War breaks out. Marilla attempts to become a nurse. Is turned down because of age and inexperience. Sends all her extra income to soldiers.
1863	►	May 19, marries John Ricker of Madbury, NH. They settle in Dover, NH.
1868	►	John Ricker dies. Marilla becomes independently wealthy.
1869	►	Attends the National Women's Suffrage Association convention.
1870	►	Attempts to vote in local NH elections. Is turned away.
1871	►	Attempts to vote again. Is once more refused. Tries to vote in every election for nearly fifty years. Lodges a protest each time she pays her property taxes.
1872	►	Travels to Germany to study the ideas of "Freethinkers."
1876	►	Returns and settles in Washington, DC where she studies law.
1882	►	May 12, admitted to bar of Washington, DC.
1889	►	Petitions state of NH to allow her to practice law. She is refused.
1890	►	Brings her case to court and wins. NH bar is opened to all women.
1891	►	Becomes 9th female member of the US Supreme Court bar. Being a member meant Marilla could argue cases before the Supreme Court.
1897	►	Applies to become Ambassador to Columbia. Is turned down.
1910	►	Announces candidacy for Governor of NH. Is not allowed to run.
1920	►	August, The 19th Amendment, giving women the right to vote, is passed. November 12th, Marilla dies.

Learn More About the Fight for Women's Rights

- Bolden, Tonya. *33 Things Every Girl Should Know About Women's History: From Suffragettes to Skirt Lengths to the E. R. A.* (Crown 2002).

- Ash, Maureen. *The Story of the Women's Movement.* (Children's Press, 1990).

Websites:

- Stories about the struggles of women, children and minorities to gain their civil rights:
  http://pbskids.org/wayback/civilrights/index.html

- Stories of women who broke barriers, and interviews by kids with women of today:
  http://teacher.scholastic.com/activities/suffrage/history.htm

Glossary

ambassador (am BASS uh dur) The top person sent by a government to represent it in another country.

ballot (BAL uht) A secret way of voting such as by machine or on a slip of paper.

bar exam (BAR eg ZAM) The test a person must pass in order to be allowed to practice law.

suffragette (suhf rij ET) Name given to women who worked for the right to vote.

— 8 —
Marian MacDowell:
An Ordinary Woman

by Barbara Turner

"*I* can't do it, Marian," Grandmother said. "You must tell your father."

She prodded eight year-old Marian toward the door. Scared, Marian waited. How could she tell Papa? What should she say?

The door opened. Papa rushed inside. Marian stared at him, alone and small.

"What is the matter?" he asked.

Marian took a deep breath and did what had to be done. "She's dead, Papa. Mama is dead."

Papa fell to his knees. Marian ran to comfort him.

· · · · ৩৩ · · · ·

Marian spent a lifetime doing what needed to be done. She was born Marian Nevins on November 22, 1857. She had two older brothers and two younger sisters. After her mother died in childbirth, Marion took over many of the household chores. Someone had to, and she was the oldest girl.

Marian grew and began to play piano. Her Aunt Caroline, a piano teacher, saw she had talent. She gave Marian lessons. In 1880, Marian went to Germany to study. When she arrived, her teacher was away on a concert tour. A friend suggested she study with Edward MacDowell, a famous American **composer**. Marian didn't want to. She had come to Europe to study under Clara Schumann, a great piano **virtuoso**, not an American. Her friend insisted, and Marian gave in. Soon, she and Edward became more than teacher and student. On July 21, 1884, they married.

Marian felt her husband's **career** was more important than her own. She said, "I hadn't been married three months before I knew that I had to make a choice between a husband and a career."

In 1896, Marian bought Hillcrest Farm in Peterborough, NH. It was a summer home where Edward could compose without interruptions. Edward loved the farm. He thought all artists needed a place to work away from everyday life. He shared his idea with Marian. Together, they decided to create an **artists' colony**. Wealthy friends like President Grover Cleveland and Andrew Carnegie donated money, and the MacDowell Colony was started. The first artists arrived in 1907.

One year later, Edward died and the money ran out. Marian did not want to see Edward's dream die with him. She did what

TIDBITS

Marian consented to marry Edward on one condition. He must devote his time to composing music and live off her inheritance for the next five years. Edward didn't like his wife supporting him, but he loved Marian and agreed.

◆—◆

In her quest to raise money for the colony, Marian said, "I hate to admit it, but women do most of it. Five music **sororities** helped me, but not one **fraternity**."

TIDBITS

During World War I, the MacDowell Colony took in the war wounded who needed a place to regain their health. During World War II, they took in foreign artists unable to return home to their own war torn countries.

•◆•

In 1940, the US Post Office put Edward MacDowell's portrait on a five cent stamp. 70,000 orders were placed.

needed to be done. She began **lecturing**, and at one event, someone asked her to play. Marian hadn't played in public in twenty-two years. Still, she played. She chose a piece written by her husband. The audience loved it!

For the next twenty-five years, Marian played her husband's music all across America and raised over $100,000.00 for the colony. What started as one log cabin on 75 acres of woodland, grew to 32 **studios** on 450 acres. Marian got the colony through the Great Depression, two world wars, and the hurricane of 1938. Because of her hard work, over 5,500 writers, musicians, and other artists have had a quiet, peaceful **environment** to work in.

Marian died on August 23, 1956, at age 98. Today, the colony she started is still alive and strong. In 2007, it celebrated its 100th anniversary. Marian made it happen. She said of herself, "I am a very ordinary woman who saw an opportunity–and I seized it."

The first sheet of stamps honoring Edward MacDowell was sold to Marian MacDowell at a ceremony on May 13,1940. Later, Marian played a piano solo to mark the occasion.

Timeline: Marian Nevins MacDowell

1857 ➤ November 22, Marian Griswold Nevins is born to David H. Nevins, a Wall Street banker, and his wife Cornelia L. Perkins, in New York, NY.

1865 ➤ Her mother dies in childbirth.

1880 ➤ Marian goes to Germany to study piano under Clara Schumann. She ends up studying under American Composer Edward MacDowell.

1884 ➤ July 21, Marian and Edward marry in Waterford, CT.

1896 ➤ Marian buys Hillcrest Farm, a summer home, in Peterborough, NH as a place for Edward to work undisturbed. Their main residence is in NY.

1904 ➤ Edward resigns as head of the Music Department at Columbia University. He becomes ill and his mind begins to fail.

1907 ➤ Marian transfers her deed to Hillcrest Farm to the newly formed Edward MacDowell Association, an artists' colony. The colony opens that summer.

1908 ➤ January 23, Edward dies. Marian resumes her career as a pianist and begins touring to raise funds for the colony.

1923 ➤ Marian is awarded a $5,000 Annual Achievement award from Pictorial Review as the American woman who made the most valuable contribution to American life that year.

1930 ➤ She receives an honorary degree from the University of NH, Durham.

1938 ➤ A hurricane destroys much of the colony. For the next two years, Marian rebuilds.

➤ She receives an honorary degree from NJ State College for Women.

1940 ➤ Marian receives the Pettee Medal from the University of NH for her valuable contributions to the state of New Hampshire.

1941 ➤ She receives the Henry Hadley medal for outstanding service to American music.

1952 ➤ August 15 is declared Marian MacDowell Day in Peterborough, NH.

1954 ➤ Hallmark Hall of Fame portrays her life story in *Lady in the Wings*.

➤ She is honored by the National Institute for Arts and Letters.

1956 ➤ August 23, Marian dies at age 98, at a friend's house in Los Angeles.

Learn More About Women in Music

- Ransom, Candice F. *Maria Von Trapp: Beyond the Sound of Music (Trailblazer Biography)*. Carolrhoda Books, 2002.
- Reich, Susanna. *Clara Schumann: Piano Virtuoso.* Clarion, 2005.
- Houston, Scott. *Play Piano in a Flash for Kids!* Hyperion, 2006.

Websites:

- The MacDowell Colony's website:
  http://www.macdowellcolony.org/history.html
- Create your own tunes on a thumb piano:
  http://www.pbskids.org/africa/piano/haveflash.html

Glossary

artists' colony (AR tistss KOL uh nee) A quiet place for writers, musicians, painters, and other artists to work.

composer (cuhm POZE uhr) A person who writes music.

environment (en VYE ruhn muhnt) The natural world of the land, sea, and air.

fraternity (fruh TUHR nuh tee) An organization of men who share a common interest.

lecturing (LEK chur ing) Giving a talk to a group in order to teach something.

sorority (suh ROHR i tee) A social club for women.

studios (STOO dee ohz) Rooms or building in which artists or photographers work.

virtuoso (vur choo OH soh) A highly skilled performer, especially a musician.

— 9 —
Mary Bradish Titcomb,
She Worked Hard at Her Craft

by Diane Mayr

She signed her early paintings "Mary Bradish Titcomb." But Mary found that women artists were not taken seriously. She changed the way she signed her paintings. First it was "M. Bradish Titcomb." Then she shortened it to "M. B. Titcomb." Viewers of her pictures wouldn't know if a man or a woman had painted them. Her work appeared in many **galleries**. Without a woman's name attached to it, there was no fear of **prejudice**.

In 1915, Mary received news. The president of the United States, Woodrow Wilson, had bought one of her paintings. The "**Portrait of Geraldine J.**" would hang in the White House. A Boston newspaper reported that Miss Titcomb "works hard at her craft."

. . . . ꧁ . . . .

TIDBITS

In 1890, Mary's salary as a teacher was $1,000 a year.

•◆•

Boston, during the late 1800s, had an active social scene. Mary attended lectures, exhibits, and artists' festivals, which included elaborate costumes.

Mary Bradish Titcomb was born in Windham, New Hampshire in 1858. Her father was a businessman. Her mother was a teacher. By the time she was seventeen, Mary was teaching school in Windham. After her mother died, Mary moved to Boston where she took classes in education. She then became an art teacher in Brockton, Massachusetts.

During her time teaching, she kept up her own art work. Her sketches received prizes. She spent her summers drawing in the White Mountains of New Hampshire. She vacationed in Europe and visited her brother out west. After 14 years, though, she decided to stop teaching. She became a full-time artist.

Mary wanted to improve her artwork, so she moved to Boston. She studied at the Museum School. One of her teachers was Edmund C. Tarbell. Tarbell was an American **impressionist** artist. Mary also went to Europe to work and study. In Paris she learned more about impressionism. She learned about color. She practiced her brush strokes. Mary worked hard at her craft.

In Boston, Mary painted in a studio called Copley Hall. She lived there, too. It was unusual, at the time, for a woman to live by herself.

In the building were other artists. Mary became friends with a group of talented women artists. In the early 1900s, women could not join certain art clubs. They could not show their works in all galleries. In 1917, Mary and her friends got together. They showed their works as a group. They became known as "The Group."

Titcomb painted portraits in her studio in Boston. She also had studios in Provincetown and Gloucester, Massachusetts. In these she painted colorful **landscapes**. She traveled to other parts of the United States. In Nogales, Arizona, she visited her brother Edward and his family. She painted the western desert and its people.

Mary's work was shown and sold all over the United States. Her most famous sale was to President Woodrow Wilson.

As she grew older, Mary developed heart disease. She died in 1927 in Marblehead, Massachusetts. Mary's belongings were sent to her brother's family in Arizona. Sadly, a warehouse fire destroyed many of her paintings and her papers. Today, Mary's "Portrait of Geraldine J." hangs in the Woodrow Wilson House in Washington, D. C.

TIDBITS

The price President Wilson paid for "Portrait of Geraldine J." may have been as much as $1500. (According to Mary's niece).

⚊•⚊

Forty years after her death, Mary's nephew added a new stone to her grave. It is inscribed, "A GREAT PAINTER AND MOST KINDLY PERSON".

Portrait of Geraldine J.

Timeline: Mary Bradish Titcomb

1858	Mary is born on September 27, in Windham, New Hampshire.
1863	Her brother, Edward, is born.
1870	Her father, Edward Titcomb, dies.
1875	Begins teaching in Windham.
1885	Her mother, Sarah Jane Abbott Titcomb, dies.
1886	Leaves New Hampshire to continue her education at the Massachusetts Normal Art School in Boston. After a one year of training, accepts a job as "Director of Drawing" in Brockton, Massachusetts.
1895	Travels to Paris, France to study art.
1901–1902	Resigns from teaching and begins studying at Museum of Fine Arts.
1909	Finishes her studies at the Museum School. Returns to Europe. Continues her studies in France and other countries
1913	Has her first **solo** exhibit of her work.
1915	President Woodrow Wilson buys the "Portrait of Geraldine J."
1917	Becomes part of "The Group." These women exhibit their work together until 1919.
1920	Buys a house in Marblehead, Massachusetts.
1927	Dies of heart disease on October 2, in Marblehead. Is buried in Windham, New Hampshire.

Learn More about Mary Bradish Titcomb, Art, and Artists of her time

- Casey, Carolyn. *Mary Cassatt ("Artist Biographies" series)*. Enslow, 2004.
- Knapp, Ruthie. *Off the Wall Museum Guides for Kids: French Impressionist Art.* Davis, 1998.
- Raimundo, Joyce. *Picture This! Activities and Adventures in Impressionism.* Watson-Guptill, 2004.

Websites:

- To see examples of art by Mary Bradish Titcomb, visit the website:

  http://www.askart.com. In the artist search type Titcomb. On the next page, at the top, left, click on "Examples of her work."

- *The National Museum of Women in the Arts.* This page will lead you to information about American women artists of the 20th century: http://www.nmwa.org/collection/20th_century.asp

Glossary

galleries (GAL uh reez) Places where paintings, sculptures, photographs and other works of art are displayed for people to see.

impressionist (im PRESH uhn ist) An artist who paints in the impressionist style. Impressionism came about in the late 1800s. Artists used small brush strokes of primary colors to imitate reflected light.

landscape (LAND skape) A painting or drawing that shows a view of land that can be seen in one place.

portrait (POR trit or POR trayt) A photograph, drawing, or painting of a person.

prejudice (PREJ uh diss) A fixed, unreasonable, or unfair opinion about someone based on the person's race, religion, or other characteristic.

solo (SOH loh) Something done by one person.

Caroline Gardner Clark Bartlett:
Nurse or Spy?

by Andrea Murphy

*A*t least a thousand broken men filled the hospital. Men with crushed legs and blinded eyes. Men covered in blood and body lice. World War I raged on as Caroline and one other nurse struggled to care for the injured soldiers.

Caroline pushed back her purple **cloak**. She knelt beside a wounded man. She tore the hem of her long skirt into strips and sang softly as she bound the soldier's wounds. Her tender care calmed the French soldier. Caroline's beautiful voice cut through the man's pain.

It was all she could do for now, but it was not enough. Caroline knew she needed to get more help.

· · · · ᧚ · · · ·

Caroline was born in LaGrange, Ohio around 1870. She was adopted by Mr. and Mrs. Curtis Clark of Rochester, New York when she was 3 years old.

As Caroline grew, so did her voice. Her clear **soprano** soared in church. It rang out at parties. Caroline became known as a gifted singer.

Caroline married Dr. James Bartlett, a dentist, around 1898. They bought a summer home in Warner, New Hampshire. Caroline started a singing school there.

Caroline talked to scientists about singing. She exchanged letters with Thomas Edison about voice. Caroline made up her own way to teach people to sing. She called it the *natural voice* **method**.

Caroline's husband died in 1909. She moved to New York City and started another singing school. She taught poor children how to sing. Caroline began singing in public again.

In 1914, Caroline moved to London, England. She set up a singing tour. Before the tour started, World War I broke out. London filled with **refugees** from Belgium. They were trying to escape the war. They had no places to live. They had no food to eat.

Caroline decided to do something. She walked around London and asked people to help. People gave her money, clothes and food for the refugees.

A doctor saw what Caroline was doing. He asked her to go to France to open a hospital for wounded soldiers. He told her to wear clothes that people would recognize so she could pass safely in the war zone. She had a purple cloak made.

Caroline put on her new cloak. She sailed across the English Channel to France. She saw hungry children and wounded soldiers. She knew she had to do more.

Caroline sailed back to England. She raised money and supplies for the hospital. She sailed back and forth across the

TIDBITS

Caroline's music school in Warner was called *Sunny Hill.*

Caroline once spoke to an audience of 140,000 ship builders in Newcastle, England to raise money for the refugees and injured soldiers.

channel dozens of times. Soldiers recognized Caroline in her purple cloak and let her pass. They called her Sister Beatrice.

Some people were jealous of Caroline. They lied about her. They said she was stealing the money she raised for the soldiers. They told people to stop giving Caroline money. They even said Caroline was a German spy.

This made Caroline feel horrible. She spent the rest of her life fighting those lies. In 1929, she moved back to Warner, New Hampshire. Her health was poor. She lost many of her friends. She had a hard time finding work.

Caroline died on February 16, 1938 in Warner. She asked that her purple cloak be sent to her hometown in Ohio. But Caroline stayed in New Hampshire. She is buried with her husband in Warner.

Caroline Bartlett as Sister Beatrice.

Timeline: Caroline Gardner Clark Bartlett

c1868 ➤ Caroline is born "Caroline Gott" in LaGrange, Ohio. Her parents are very poor. She is adopted around age 3 by the Clarks of Rochester, NY

c1890 ➤ Caroline starts singing professionally.

c1898 ➤ Caroline marries Dr. James Bartlett, a man some 30 years older than she.

c1899 ➤ The Bartletts buy a house in Warner, NH. Caroline starts a summer singing school there.

1907 ➤ Lillian Nordica, a premier **diva** of the time, begins training with Caroline.

1909 ➤ Caroline's husband dies. Lillian Nordica invites Caroline to come to NYC and helps her establish a singing school.

1914 ➤ Caroline plans to tour England singing with Nordica.

May, Nordica dies before she can join Caroline for the tour.

July, Caroline is living in London when World War I breaks out. Touched by the flood of Belgian refugees, she raises funds to help them. She starts wearing her **trademark** purple cloak and becomes known as Sister Beatrice.

November, The French military ask Caroline to open a hospital. Within two months the hospital at Yvetot is up and running and Caroline is appointed hospital director.

1915 ➤ October, Caroline is accused of mishandling the monies raised for the hospital and is dismissed as its director. She is accused of being a spy.

1918 ➤ Despite attempts to discredit her, Caroline continues working in the war relief effort. She raises hundreds of thousands of dollars for the Serbian's Widows and Orphans fund.

1919 ➤ With the war over, Caroline's relief work ends with her reputation in tatters. As a result, she finds it difficult to find paying work. Caroline spends the rest of her life trying to clear her name.

1929 ➤ Caroline settles permanently in Warner, NH.

1938 ➤ February 16, Caroline dies in Warner, NH.

NOTE: c1890 means about or around 1890

Learn More About Caroline Gardner Clark Bartlett, Music, and World War I

- Belman, Felice and Pride, Mike (editors). *The New Hampshire Century.* University Press of New England, 2001.

- Husain, Shahrukh. *The Barefoot Book of Stories from the Opera.* Barefoot Books, 1999.

- Granfield, Lina. *Where Poppies Grow: A World War I Companion.* Fitzhenry & Whiteside, Ltd., 2005

- Zeinert, Karen. *Those Extraordinary Women of World War I.* Lerner Publishing Group, 2001.

Websites:

- A Short World War I History: http://www.spartacus.schoolnet.co.uk/FWW.htm
- Sing-Along Songs: http://kids.niehs.nih.gov./music.htm
- The Art of Singing by Luisa Tetrazzini and Enrico Caruso: http://www.ibiblio.org/ebooks/Tetrazzini/Art_Singing.htm

Glossary

cloak (klohk) a loose coat with no sleeves worn wrapped around the shoulders and fastened at the neck.

diva (DEE vah) The star female singer in an opera company.

method (METH uhd) a way of doing something.

refugees (REF yuh jeez) people forced to leave their country because of war, persecution, or a natural disaster.

soprano (suh PRAN oh) the highest singing voice. A person who sings in a soprano voice.

trademark (TRADE mark) A sign or mark by which a person becomes known.

Persis Foster Eames Albee:

Business Pioneer

by Andrea Murphy

Persis Albee put on her hat. She took one last glance in the mirror. She had to look her best. She needed people to let her into their homes. She needed them to buy the books she was selling. Persis was alone in the world with her children. It's never easy for a woman to raise children alone. In 1881, it was almost impossible.

· · · · ◌ · · · ·

Persis Foster Eames was born in Newry, Maine in 1836. Her father, Alexander, farmed the rocky soil. Her mother, Miranda, cared for their growing family.

Persis married Ellery Albee in 1866. They lived in Winchester, New Hampshire. Persis was president of the Winchester **Literary Guild**. Ellery was a lawyer. He became a state senator, and treasurer of the local bank.

In 1868, Persis had a son, named Elbert. He lived only one day. Two years later, her second son, Ellery, was born. In 1873, she had daughter Ellen.

Persis and her husband opened a general store in their home. The store was a big success. Persis became known as a smart businesswoman.

Book seller David McConnell visited Persis's store in 1879. He could see that Persis was a great salesperson. He asked her to sell books for him. Persis became a part-time **depot agent**. She sold books door-to-door. McConnell later said Persis was one of the most successful agents he had.

In March 1881, Persis's husband went to jail. He had stolen over $100,000 from his bank. A local newspaper wrote that the town "was shaken from center to **circumference**" by this.

Ellery spent many long years in jail. Persis was left alone to care for her children. Her business skills helped get her through these hard times.

David McConnell started the California Perfume Company in 1886. He put Persis in charge of sales. For six months, Persis was his only worker. She sold perfume door-to-door. She did such a good job, McConnell made her a manager. Persis traveled all over, hiring women to work as depot agents. She trained them to sell door-to-door. The company grew.

By 1903, the company had over 10,000 depot agents. That same year, McConnell wrote *The History of the California Perfume Company*. He said that Persis was an important part of his early years in business. He called her the "Mother of the

California Perfume Company."

Persis retired around 1912. She moved into her daughter's home. Persis died on December 7, 1914, and is buried in Winchester, New Hampshire.

That is not the end of Persis's story. In 1939, the California Perfume Company got a new name – Avon. More than 40 million women have sold for Avon. Persis was the first, and one of the best.

Since 1969, Avon has given awards to its top salespeople. The award is a statue of Persis. Women in over 140 countries have received The Albee Award.

More than 100 years after Persis sold her first bottle of perfume, Avon teamed up with Mattel to make a very special doll. The Mrs. P.F.E. Albee Barbie Doll has been a favorite with **collectors** since 1997. Persis never could have imagined this!

TIDBITS

Persis was said to be widowed by 1885. Her husband Ellery was, in fact, still alive in 1920. According to the census taken that year, he was living in the same New York town as his son.

•◆•

Persis's name has been written using several different spellings – Persis, Persus, and Perseus!

Barbie® as Mrs. P.F.E. Albee

Timeline: Persis Foster Eames Albee

1836 ▶	May 30, Persis Foster Eames is born the seventh of eleven children to Alexander and Miranda Eames in Newry, Maine.
1866 ▶	December 20, marries Attorney Ellery Albee and moves to Winchester, NH.
1868 ▶	Son Elbert is born. He lives one day.
1870 ▶	Son Ellery Eames Albee is born.
1873 ▶	Daughter Ellen Eames Albee is born.
c1877 ▶	Persis and Ellery open a general store in their home.
1879 ▶	Persis sells books door-to-door for David McConnell, a salesman for a New York company.
1881 ▶	Husband Ellery goes to jail for stealing from the Ashuelot Savings Bank.
1886 ▶	Persis starts selling perfume for McConnell, who has founded California Perfume Company.
1903 ▶	McConnell gives Persis the honorary title of "Mother of the California Perfume Company" in recognition of her method of recruiting and training salespeople.
1912 ▶	Persis's health forces her to retire. She moves into daughter Ellen's home in Baldwinville, Massachusetts.
1914 ▶	December 7, Persis dies in Templeton, Massachusetts at age 78. She is buried in Winchester, New Hampshire.
1969 ▶	Avon, Inc. begins using Persis's likeness on the dolls and statues it awards its employees.
1997 ▶	Mattel, Inc. creates a Barbie Doll for Avon. The doll, named Mrs. P.F.E. Albee, honors Persis's contribution to the company.
2006 ▶	The Sheridan House Museum in Winchester, New Hampshire dedicates a memorial plaque to Persis.

NOTE: c1877 means around or about 1877.

Learn More about Persis Albee and the Beauty Industry

- Krohn, Katherine E. *Madam C. J. Walker: Pioneer Business Woman.* Capstone Press, 2006.

- Lasky, Kathryn. *Vision of Beauty: The Story of Sarah Breedlove Walker*. Candlewick, 2003.

- Shuker, Nancy. *Elizabeth Arden (Giants of American Industry)*. Blackbirch Press, 2001.

- Epstein, Rachel. *Estee Lauder: Beauty Business Success (Book Report Biographies)*. Franklin Watts, 2000.

- Older, Jules. *Anita!: The Woman Behind the Body Shop*. Charlesbridge Publishing, 1998.

Website:

- The Historical Society of Cheshire County. Persis Foster Eames Albee: The First "Avon Lady." by Vicki E. D. Flanders: http://www.hsccnh.org/educationhp/hp8.cfm

Glossary

circumference – (sur KUHM fur uhnss) The outer edge of a circle.

collectors – (kuhl LEK tuhrz) People who gather things together, such as dolls, coins, or stamps, as a hobby.

depot agents – Salespeople who sold goods door-to-door. They did not sell outside of the area in which they lived, and they usually lived in a town with a railroad depot.

guild – (GILD) A group or organization of people who do the same kind of work or have the same interests.

literary – (lit uhr AIR ee) Having to do with novels, plays, short stories, poems, and essays. A literary guild is a club that reads and discusses literature.

Elizabeth Gurley Flynn:
Fighting Injustice

by Diane Mayr

Elizabeth Gurley Flynn was five when her family moved to the mill city of Manchester, New Hampshire. Here the mills "stretched like prisons along the banks of the Merrimac River." Lizzie saw the effects of being poor. "I hate poverty," she later wrote. She remembered her Manchester neighbors. The children "were without underwear, even in the coldest weather."

The short time she spent in Manchester made a lasting impression on Elizabeth. She saw women work long hours to support their families on one dollar a day. She saw children working. She knew that rich mill owners were taking advantage of the poor workers. Elizabeth Gurley Flynn would work the rest of her life to change things.

· · · · ‾ · · · ·

Elizabeth was born in Concord, New Hampshire in 1890. Her mother was a seamstress. She encouraged her four children to read. Her father a **civil engineer**. He taught the children about **injustice**.

The family was poor. Lizzie's father traveled to find work. When she was 10, the whole family moved to New York. In New York, too, workers were treated badly and paid poorly. People lived in unhealthy housing.

Lizzie attended **protest** meetings with her parents. She tried public speaking. She became very good at it. At age 16, she was arrested for speaking without a permit. It was Elizabeth's first arrest. Lizzie left high school the next year. Reading and living would complete her education. She was ready to start her life's work—fighting injustice.

The International Workers of the World sent her to New England in 1912. She went to help the workers in the Lawrence, Massachusetts labor strike.

The weather was cold when the strike began. The strikers were making no money, so families couldn't buy food. There were violent attacks by the police. Lawrence was a dangerous place for children. Elizabeth took some of the strikers' children to New York City. They were cared for until the strike was over.

Workers in Lawrence came from 25 nations. Many were recent **immigrants** and needed help. Elizabeth took on the job. She fought for rights such as freedom of speech. She worked on court cases. In 1920 she helped start the American Civil Liberties Union. The A.C.L.U. wanted all people to have the rights promised by the U.S. Constitution.

After taking time off for illness, Elizabeth joined the Communist Party. She thought the Communist Party offered a way out of poverty. It gave women a chance to be equals.

TIDBITS

In 1903, 13 year-old Elizabeth won a prize from the New York Times for an essay she wrote.

•–•

Members of the I.W.W. were known as "Wobblies."

•–•

Over her lifetime, she was arrested at least 10 times!

Elizabeth would later become the first women leader of the American **Communist Party**.

Many Americans wrongly believed all Communists were dangerous. They thought that the Soviet Union (Russia), a large Communist country, wanted to conquer the world.

After World War II, people became overly afraid of the "threat of Communism." They did many unjust things. People suspected of being Communists were "blacklisted." The names of those persons were put on a list. If your name was on the list, you could lose your job, or not be hired if you needed a job. Some people changed their names and went into hiding.

Elizabeth was arrested for planning to overthrow the U.S. government. She had read many books. She read one called *The Communist Manifesto*. For some people this was proof enough that she was guilty. Her writings were also used against her.

Flynn entered prison in January 1955. Much of her time was spent in the library. She told a friend, "I've read over 200 books. . ." Twenty-eight months later she was let out.

She kept on working, but by 1964, she was getting old. Elizabeth went to Russia to rest and to write her autobiography. Elizabeth Gurley Flynn became ill after only one month. She died on September 5. The story of her life was never completed.

Elizabeth Gurley Flynn was jailed for her beliefs.

Timeline: Elizabeth Gurley Flynn

1890 ➤ August 7, born in Concord, New Hampshire.

1895 ➤ The Flynn family moves to Manchester, New Hampshire.

1900 ➤ The family permanently settles in the South Bronx, New York.

1906 ➤ January 31, gives her first public speech.
August, she and her father are arrested.
Joins the International Workers of the World.

1907 ➤ Takes part in her first strike in Bridgeport, Connecticut.
Fall, does not return to high school.
December, visits Iowa iron mines. Falls in love with John Archibald Jones, a miner and organizer.

1908 ➤ Marries Jack Jones. In the fall, her first child, a boy, dies at birth.

1909–1910 ➤ She is jailed and writes a description of the poor treatment of prisoners.
May 19, 1910, her son, Fred (called Buster), is born in New York City.
Her marriage ends.

1912 ➤ The "Bread and Roses" strike, Lawrence, Massachusetts. Flynn leads the "Lawrence Children's Crusade."

1913 ➤ Participates in the Paterson, New Jersey silk workers strike.

1920 ➤ Helps to found the American Civil Liberties Union (A.C.L.U.).

1926–1936 ➤ Has a mental and physical collapse due to overworking. She spends 10 years in Portland, Oregon recovering.

1937 ➤ Returns to New York to take care of her sick mother. Joins the Communist Party.

1940 ➤ Her only son, Fred, dies.

1941–1945 ➤ During World War II helps the war effort. Encourages women to go to work. She pressures the government to give women childcare, transportation, and equal pay.

1951 ➤ June 20, Flynn is arrested as a Communist. After a 10 month trial she is found guilty.

1955 ➤ January, after several unsuccessful appeals, Flynn enters prison.

1961 ➤ Becomes the first woman leader of the Communist Party in the U.S.

1964 ➤ September 5, dies in Moscow, Russia. She is given an elaborate state funeral. Her ashes are returned to the U.S. and buried in Chicago, Illinois.

Learn More About Elizabeth Gurley Flynn and Labor Strikes

- Baker, Julie. *Bread and Roses Strike of 1912 (American Workers)*. Morgan Reynolds Publishing, 2007.

- Bartoletti, Susan Campbell. *Kids on Strike!* Houghton Mifflin, 2003.

- Paterson, Katherine. *Bread and Roses, Too.* Houghton Mifflin, 2006.

Websites:

- Elizabeth Gurley Flynn's speech from her trial in 1952 is found here. It is number 89: http://www.americanrhetoric.com/speeches/elizabethgurleyflynn.htm.

- More information about the Lawrence, MA strike of 1912: http://www.massmoments.org/moment.cfm?mid = 16.

- "Elizabeth Flynn." *Sparticus Educational*: http://www.spartacus.schoolnet.co.uk/USAflynn.htm.

Glossary

civil engineer (CIV il en juh NIHR) An engineer trained to design and build public works like highways or dams.

Communist Party (COM yuh nist PAR tee) The main political party of the former Soviet Union (now Russia) that believed in organizing the country so that all land, housing, factories, and so forth belong to the government or community and the profits are shared by all.

immigrants (IM uh gruhnts) People who come from abroad to live permanently in a country.

injustice (in JUHSS tiss) An unfair situation or action.

protest (PROH test) A demonstration or statement against something such as a war protest.

— 13 —
Lotte Jacobi:
Artist and Photographer

by M. Lu Major

$\mathcal{L}$otte stood on the deck of the great ship. The *Georgic* was sailing to America. Lotte was leaving behind the life she had always known. For two years, Adolf Hitler had been in power. Life in Germany had become a nightmare for anyone of Jewish **descent,** as Lotte was.

Lotte would stay with her sister, Ruth, in New York City. She did not want to leave her home, but she could not live without her art.

· · · · ◠◡ · · · ·

Johanna Alexandra Jacobi was born in Thorn, West Prussia in 1896. Her family called her Lotte (LOT uh).

Four **generations** of Lotte's family had been photographers. Lotte said that such a family tree meant "I was to be a photographer and that was that."

When she was twelve years old Lotte asked her father for a camera. He told her to make one. He wanted her to understand how photography

TIDBITS

The town where Lotte Jacobi was born is now part of Poland.

worked. She made a pin-hole camera. "It occurred to me," Lotte said later, "that this camera was a sort of cage for light that controlled its effect." For the rest of her life, Lotte studied how light created pictures.

Lotte not only learned from her father. She also studied at a photography school in Munich, Germany. She became well-known in Europe for her photographs of famous people. She made pictures of artists, actors, and **politicians**.

When Lotte was 20 she married. The next year she had a son. Her marriage soon ended and Lotte was left to support her son.

Photography was not Lotte's only interest. She also loved travel. In 1932 Lotte went to Russia. She stayed for nearly three months. While she was away, things changed in Germany. The Nazi party came into power. Adolf Hitler and his people began to **persecute** the Jews. They took away their jobs. They made Jewish people wear yellow stars on their clothes so they could be identified easily. They forced many to move into **segregated** neighborhoods.

Lotte's father became ill and died. Lotte knew it was time to leave Germany. She and her mother packed as many of Lotte's pictures as they could. But the pictures were on **glass plates**. Thousands of plates were too heavy to carry. Most of them were lost forever.

Lotte settled in New York City and worked there for twenty years. In 1940 she married her second husband, Erich Reiss. During that time, Lotte invented a new kind of art called photogenics. The pictures were made without a camera. Lotte used only a flashlight on photo paper "as you would draw," she wrote, "with a brush." She created modern, beautiful designs. Lotte was not sure, at first, if these pictures could be called art. Erich Reiss urged his wife to continue to produce the lovely works.

Erich Reiss died in 1951. In 1955, Lotte moved to Deering, New Hampshire. She opened a new studio. Lotte not only took photographs, she also showed pictures by other photographers. She became involved in politics. At the 1976 Democratic National **Convention**, Lotte was the oldest person with a press pass. The pass allowed her to photograph anywhere in the convention hall.

Lotte believed that every day should be filled with learning. "Never stop dreaming!" she once said. "One's heart is never content with the photographs made, one always knows a better one can be made."

Lotte Jacobi died in 1990. Her photos continue to appear in exhibits all over the world.

TIDBITS

After she moved to New Hampshire, Lotte gardened, raised bees, and took classes at the University of New Hampshire.

One of Lotte Jacobi's "photogenics." The background was done with a flashlight on light-sensitive paper. The hand and dancer were added later.

Timeline: Lotte Jacobi

1896	➤	August 17, Johanna Alexandra Jacobi is born in Thorn, West Prussia (now Poland).
1916	➤	May 18, marries Fritz Honig.
1917	➤	Gives birth to her son, John.
1920	➤	The Jacobi family moves to Berlin, Germany.
1924	➤	Lotte's marriage ends.
1925–1927	➤	Attends the Bavarian State Academy of Photography in Munich, Germany.
1932	➤	October, to January, 1933, Lotte travels to Russia to take photos.
1933	➤	Adolf Hitler comes to power in Germany.
1935	➤	Lotte's father dies. September, leaves Germany for America. Opens a portrait studio in New York City.
1940	➤	October 7, marries publisher Erich Reiss in New York City.
1947	➤	Lotte invents a camera-less type of abstract art: photogenics.
1951	➤	Erich Reiss dies of a heart attack.
1955	➤	Lotte, her son, and his wife move to Deering, New Hampshire.
1974	➤	The University of New Hampshire awards Lotte an honorary degree, Doctor of Fine Arts.
1976	➤	Lotte is the oldest working photographer at the Democratic National Convention.
1977	➤	January, attends the inauguration of President Jimmy Carter. March, visits Peru.
1979	➤	Lotte changes her name legally from Johanna Reiss to Lotte Johanna Jacobi Reiss.
1989	➤	NH State Council on the Arts initiates the Lotte Jacobi Living Treasure Award. It is given every two years to an artist who makes a significant contribution to his/her art.
1990	➤	May 6, dies in Concord, New Hampshire.

Learn More about Lotte Jacobi and Women in Photography

- Keller, Emily. *Margaret Bourke-White: A Photographer's Life*. Minneapolis: Lerner Publications, 1996.

- Martin W. Sandler. *America Through the Lens: Photographers Who Changed the Nation*. New York: Henry Holt, 2005.

- Sullivan, George. *Berenice Abbott, Photographer: An Independent Vision*. New York: Clarion, 2006.

Websites:

- The University of New Hampshire Milne Special Collection: http://www.izaak.unh.edu/specoll/mancoll/jacobi.htm

- New Hampshire State Council on the Arts: http://www.nh.gov/nharts/artsandartists/inmemory/lottejacobi.html

- How to Make a Pinhole Camera: http://www.exploratorium.edu/light_walk/camera_todo.html

Glossary

convention (kuhn VEN shuhn) A large gathering of people who have the same interests, such as a political meeting where candidates are chosen.

descent (di SENT) a family line.

generations (JEN uh RAY shuhnz) Family members who share an ancestor.

glass plates (GLASS PLAYTSS) panes of glass coated with a light-sensitive chemical. The plates were large, 20 inches by 24 inches.

persecute (PUR suh kyoot) To treat someone cruelly and unfairly.

politicians (pol uh TISH uhnz) People who run for or hold public office, such as a senator.

segregated (SEG ruh GAY tuhd) Kept apart from the main group.

Bernice Blake Perry:
New Hampshire's Queen of the Air

by Janet Buell

The **form letter** was dated 1933 and began "Dear Sir". At 5 feet 4 inches and 110 pounds, Bernice Blake was no "sir". She was a cute, strong-minded woman.

Bernice had already logged the 200 solo flight hours she needed. On test day she had hopped into the airplane and took off. She showed the tester **spot landings**, spins, and 360 degree turns. On the written test, she answered questions about math, engines, navigation, and airplane construction.

The "Dear Sir" letter made it official. She had become New England's first female **transport** airline **pilot**. Bernice was on her way to becoming New Hampshire's Queen of the Air.

· · · · ⌒ · · · ·

In the very early days of **aviation**, only men flew. That fact changed by the mid 1910s and early 1920s. A handful of daring women took to the skies. Bernice was one of the first wave of women to follow.

Her mother had died when Bernice was a young girl. Bernice helped raise her two younger sisters. She also worked at her family's **creamery**.

Bernice studied music at the New England Conservatory after high school. There she had seen an airplane flying overhead – a rare sight in those days. Bernice set aside her dreams to be a concert pianist. She knew she had to fly.

Bernice took flight lessons at Curtiss Flying Services at Manchester airport. As part of her lessons, she worked on engines. She also spent time in the motor room and on airplane construction. In 1929, she received her private pilot's license. Bernice and a male student were the only ones out of fourteen who passed. Bernice was only 24 years old.

Bernice was good in the air. Her instructor told a newspaper reporter that Bernice could "out-fly" most men. Curtiss Flying Services hired the lively young woman to host women visitors and fliers. She also traveled around New Hampshire and Vermont talking to people about aviation.

While Bernice talked flying, people talked about Bernice. Newspapers regularly covered the spirited young aviator. Male pilots were still something of a **novelty**. A woman flier was really big news.

Until 1938, Bernice was one of only 56 women in the US to hold a transport airline pilot's license. She flew passengers. She gave flying lessons, too. Bernice wrote a column called Airport News for the *Manchester Union Leader*. She also joined the 99s. This woman's aviators' club was named after the 99 female

TIDBITS

Bernice Blake's parents owned Blake's Restaurants and Ice Cream.

•▪•

Back in the early days of aviation, you could take a quick ride on a plane for $1.00.

•▪•

In the beginning, airports didn't have blacktop runways. Most planes landed on grassy airstrips. This made it tough to land or take off during mud season.

•▪•

The first Women's Air Derby began in California on August 29, 1929.

fliers who first formed the group. One of their most famous members was Amelia Earhart.

Bernice married fellow flier, Winthrop Perry, in 1936. The couple shared a love of photography. Winthrop designed a camera holder so Bernice could snap pictures while flying. She took hundreds of **aerial** photos for the NH State Planning **Commission**. The Commission used the photos to decide where to put new airports and industrial parks.

When World War II broke out, Bernice and others had to stop flying. The military needed gasoline for the war. She and Winthrop decided to take up sailing.

The New Hampshire state police hired Bernice to take photos of accident scenes. She was also the official photographer of the MacDowell colony. There, she photographed the famous artists, writers, and musicians who came to create at the colony.

Bernice saved her money. She also played the stock market like a pro. The three million dollars she made still funds **scholarships** for deserving students in Wilton, Milford, and Lyndeboro. Many students have gone to college courtesy of Bernice Blake Perry, New Hampshire's first Queen of the Air.

The form letter Bernice received that granted her license.

Timeline: Bernice Blake Perry

1905	➤	March 2, Bernice Blake is born in Manchester, New Hampshire to Edward and Gertrude Blake.
1929	➤	May 8, Bernice gets her student permit for flight school.
1929	➤	July 15, Bernice flies solo for the first time.
1929	➤	Bernice receives her private pilot's license.
1932	➤	Bernice starts logging more nighttime flying hours in preparation for the transport license test.
1933	➤	August 31, Bernice receives her transport pilot license. She is the first woman in New England to do so.
1936	➤	October 9, Bernice Blake marries Winthrop Perry.
1938	➤	June 28, flying as a passenger, Bernice flies to Cincinnati, Ohio to pick up her new airplane, a 50 horsepower Aeronca. She flies her plane home to New Hampshire.
1938–1948	➤	Bernice takes aerial photos for the State Planning and Development Commission and for private businesses.
1948–1970s	➤	Bernice becomes an accomplished professional photographer who takes photos for several local newspapers. She also works as a **stringer** for the Associated Press.
1984	➤	until her death—Bernice hosts the annual High Hopes Balloon Festival in her back yard to raise money for terminally ill children.
1995	➤	Bernice Blake Perry takes her final flight at age 86. She doesn't take off or land the yellow Piper Cub airplane. She does fly it once it is airborne.
1996	➤	July 10, Bernice Blake Perry dies. She leaves almost $3 million to fund student scholarships.

Learn More about Bernice Blake Perry and other Women Aviators

- Atkins, Jeanine. *Wings and Rockets: The Story of Women in Air and Space*. Farrar, Straus and Giroux, 2003.

- Hopkins, Ellen. *Storming the Skies: The Story of Katherine and Marjorie Stinson, Pioneer Women Aviators*. Avisson Press, Inc. 2004.

- LaFontaine, Bruce. *Famous Women Aviators*. Dover Publications, 2001.

Websites:

- Famous Women Aviators:
  http://library. thinkquest. org/J0110426/famous/women.html

- PSB, American Experience, Fly Girls:
  http://www.pbs.org/wgbh/amex/flygirls/peopleevents/index.html

Glossary

aerial (AIR ee uhl) Happening in the air.

aviation (ay vee AY shuhn) The science of building and flying.

cockpit (KOK pit) The area in the front of a plane or boat where the pilot sits.

commission (kuh MISH uhn) A group of people who meet to solve a particular problem or do certain tasks.

creamery (KREEM uh ree) A place where dairy products are prepared and sold.

form letter (FORM LET ur) A letter in a standard form sent to large numbers of people.

navigation (NAV uh GAY shuhn) Charting a course for a plane or ship.

novelty (NOV uhl tee) Something new, interesting, and unusual.

scholarships (SKOL ur ships) Grants or prizes that pay for a person to go to college or follow a course of study.

spot landing (SPOT LAND ing) Being able to land your plane as close to a mark as possible.

stringer (STRING ur) A part time news writer or photographer.

transport pilot (TRANSS port PYE luht) This was what we now call commercial pilot. Commercial pilots are allowed to take passengers to their destinations.

—15—
Elizabeth Yates:
Newbery Award Winning Author

by M. Lu Major

"What did Mother and Father say?" Elizabeth asked her older sister, Jinny. "Will they let you teach at Smith College?"

Jinny's eyes were red and swollen. She shook her head. "Father and mother want me to be a **debutante** next year. Then I'll probably get married."

Elizabeth couldn't believe what she'd heard. Later, she wrote in her diary: *Could this happen to me? Could someone take the pencil out of my hand, tear up my notebooks, say I was to write no more?*

· · · · ◯ · · · ·

Elizabeth Yates was born in 1904 in Buffalo, New York. She was the youngest daughter in a family of seven children. Elizabeth loved to read and write stories and poems. She made up adventures about the dolls that lived in her doll house.

TIDBITS

In New York, Elizabeth supported herself as a model, a **comparison** shopper, and a babysitter.

Elizabeth's family was wealthy but she was not spoiled. Her loving yet strict parents expected each Yates child to do chores. Mrs. Yates called these household tasks "privileges." The Yates family also owned a farm in Orchard Park, New York. During World War I, many farm hands were fighting in Europe. Then the children also helped in the fields.

Elizabeth knew, even as a child, that she wanted to earn her living as a writer. Besides writing stories and poetry, she also kept a diary. In 1923, Elizabeth felt her writing was ready to be published. She sent 30 of her best poems to a publisher. One month later, the poems came back. The editor wrote: ". . . you have some excellent ideas. . . but the **mechanics** are not good." Elizabeth wasn't discouraged. She felt the letter was "a **milestone** on a long journey."

Later in the year Elizabeth took exams to enter college. She failed math. She was not really disappointed. She wanted to go to New York City and become a writer. Her parents insisted she attend a **boarding school** for one year. Elizabeth made a deal with her father. She would do her best at school. Afterwards, she wanted to get a summer job and earn money to move to New York. Her father agreed to the plan.

Elizabeth's boarding school teachers saw her talent. They arranged private writing lessons. Elizabeth's father also kept his word. The next fall she moved to New York City to try her luck.

She sent out poems, short stories, and a novel. None sold, but finally some letters said, "Try us again." Progress!

1927 was special. Elizabeth's writing began to sell. She also met Bill McGreal. They fell in love. Bill went to work in England in 1929. Elizabeth followed. They married there and stayed for 10 years. Elizabeth continued to sell short stories, articles, and encyclopedia entries. After visiting Switzerland, she wrote *High Holiday*, the first in a series of books about Michael and Meredith Lamb.

When World War II began, Elizabeth and Bill left England. They bought a house with 67 acres of woods in Peterborough, New Hampshire. They called their home **Shieling**. In 1943, Bill McGreal lost his sight. Elizabeth's writing supported them while he learned a new kind of work. Soon, Elizabeth had a dozen books to her name.

One day, Elizabeth learned the story of a former slave named Amos Fortune. He had lived in the nearby town of Jaffrey. His grave stone gave little clue to his history, but Elizabeth did careful research. Elizabeth wrote Amos's story in a novel for children. In 1951, *Amos Fortune, Free Man* was awarded the Newbery Medal. Thirty one other books followed that success.

Bill McGreal died in 1963. Elizabeth stayed at Shieling for 29 more years. She moved from there to Concord, New Hampshire. She gave her beloved Shieling Forest to the state of New Hampshire. She died on July 29, 2001.

TIDBITS

Elizabeth's first book sale was not her book at all. Elizabeth helped her younger brother Bobby write *When I Was a Harvester*. It was the story of his summer on a Canadian wheat farm.

•◆•

Elizabeth never went to college. Later she received honorary degrees from 7 colleges.

Timeline: Elizabeth Yates

1905 ➤ December 6, Born Mary Elizabeth Yates to Henry Yates, a businessman, and Mary Duffy Yates, a homemaker, in Buffalo, New York.

1915 ➤ Elizabeth receives a diary for her eleventh birthday and begins to write.

1918 ➤ America enters World War I.

1923 ➤ Elizabeth submits poems to a publisher for the first time. They are rejected.

1924 ➤ She fails the College Board math exams. Her parents send her to boarding school.

1927 ➤ April 17, meets Bill McGreal in New York City.

July 5, has a poem accepted for publication.

August 15, sells an article to a magazine and is offered a job on the staff.

1929 ➤ November 6, moves to England and marries Bill McGreal.

1930 ➤ Elizabeth's first book, *When I Was A Harvester*, written with her brother Bob, is published.

1939 ➤ Europe is at war. The McGreals return permanently to the U. S.

1941–1945 ➤ America fights in World War II. Elizabeth volunteers to be a plane spotter during the war.

1943 ➤ Bill McGreal loses his sight.

May, Elizabeth wins an award for her book, *Patterns on the Wall*.

1947 ➤ February, Elizabeth's book, *Nearby*, becomes a best seller. The McGreals use the money earned to pay off their house.

May, Bill McGreal becomes the executive director of the NH Association for the Blind.

1949 ➤ Elizabeth begins researching and writing *Amos Fortune, Free Man*.

1950 ➤ May, *Amos Fortune* wins the *Herald Tribune* Spring Festival Award.

1951 ➤ February, *Amos Fortune* is awarded the Newbery Medal.

1963 ➤ Bill McGreal dies. Elizabeth takes over his work for the NH Association for the Blind.

1992 ➤ Elizabeth moves from Peterborough to Concord, NH.

2001 ➤ Elizabeth dies in Concord at age 95.

Learn More about Elizabeth Yates and Becoming a Writer

- Naylor, Phyllis Reynolds. *How I Came to Be a Writer*. Aladdin Books, 1987.
- Yates, Elizabeth. *Spanning Time: A Diary Keeper Becomes a Writer*. Cobblestone Publishing, Inc. 1996.

Websites:

- More on Elizabeth Yates:

  http://www.elizabethyates.com
  http://www.elliemik.com/yates.html

Glossary

boarding school (BORD ing SKOOL). A school that students may live in during the school year.

comparison (kuhm PAIR i suhn) Judging one thing against another.

debutante (DAY byoo tahnt) A young woman who officially enters society for the first time.

mechanics (muh KAN iks) The technical part of an activity such as grammar in writing.

milestone (MILE stone) An important event or development.

shieling (SHEE ling) A small hut or shelter.

Elizabeth Orton Jones: Old Girl, You are an Artist!

by Andrea Murphy

Elizabeth's mother tucked her into bed. She kissed her little girl good night. The child listened as her mother's footsteps faded. When all was silent, Elizabeth pulled out a hidden piece of chalk. She stood on her bed, and began to draw on the headboard. She drew until the last light of day slipped away.

In the morning, Elizabeth did her best to erase the pictures. She lay back down and listened for her mother's footsteps. The door pushed open. Blurry pictures seemed to jump off the **headboard**. Elizabeth's mother sat on the bed, and brushed the chalk dust from her daughter's hair. She smiled, and kissed her little girl good morning.

· · · · ◎ · · · ·

Elizabeth Orton Jones was born in Highland Park, Illinois on June 25, 1910. She was the oldest of three children. Her father, George, was a violinist. Her mother, Jessie, was a writer and **pianist**.

Music, laughter, and interesting guests filled the house. When company came, Elizabeth liked to hide under the table. She loved listening to the grown-ups talk.

Elizabeth's parents encouraged their children to be creative. They asked the children to share their thoughts and ideas. They gave them silent time to read and write. They urged the children to draw and look at art.

Elizabeth never stopped drawing. She learned different ways to create art in college. She went to France to study painting. Elizabeth discovered her love for drawing children. When she returned, she had produced enough art to have a one-person show at the **Smithsonian Institution**.

Elizabeth's time in France inspired her to write and illustrate her first children's book. *Ragman of Paris and His Ragamuffins* appeared in 1937. Elizabeth would go on to publish more than 20 books.

In 1942, Elizabeth's book *Twig* came out. That same year, Elizabeth illustrated another book. She had to bring the pictures to the author in Mason, New Hampshire. She saw a run-down old house. It had no electricity, running water, or heat. She had just enough money from selling *Twig* to buy it. She named her house *Misty Meadow*. The people of Mason grew to love Elizabeth. They called her *Twig*, after the character in her book.

In 1944, Elizabeth illustrated *Prayer for a Child*. Her pictures were so wonderful, she won the 1945 **Caldecott Medal**. It made Elizabeth famous.

TIDBITS

Elizabeth loved telling people she was "born at half-past Christmas."

• ◆ •

During her acceptance speech for the 1945 Caldecott Medal, Elizabeth said, "I do not consider myself an artist. Not yet. Though I should like to be able to say . . . on the morning of my 99th birthday, 'Old girl, you are an artist!'"

An editor saw these pictures. She wanted Elizabeth to illustrate a book for her. Elizabeth wasn't interested, but the editor kept asking. Elizabeth knew she could use the money. She wanted to fix up *Misty Meadow*. She agreed to illustrate *Little Red Riding Hood* for Golden Books. Elizabeth used *Misty Meadow* as a model for some of the pictures. She used another Mason house as a model, too. That house is now *Pickety Place*.

Although Elizabeth had no children of her own, hundreds of New Hampshire girls and boys knew and loved Twig. She directed children in plays that she wrote. She helped establish a children's room in the Mason Public Library. She volunteered at New Hampshire's **Crotched Mountain Rehabilitation Center**. There she encouraged children with disabilities to draw and write. Elizabeth's volunteer work went on for close to 50 years.

Elizabeth died on May 10, 2005 in Peterborough, New Hampshire.

Pickety Place in Mason, NH. Model home for the story Little Red Riding Hood

Timeline: Elizabeth Orton Jones

1910 ➤ June 25, Elizabeth Orton Jones is the first of 3 children born to violinist George Roberts Jones and writer Jessie Mae Orton Jones in Highland Park, Illinois.

1932 ➤ March 15, graduated from the University of Chicago.
Receives a Diplôme in painting from the École des Beaux Arts in France.

1937 ➤ Oxford University Press publishes Elizabeth's first book, *Ragman of Paris and His Ragamuffins*.

1942 ➤ Buys a house she calls *Misty Meadow* in Mason, NH with her first royalty check from the book *Twig*. The house costs $2,000 – exactly the amount of her royalty check. She lives there for more than 60 years.

1944 ➤ Wins a Caldecott Honor for her illustrations of *Small Rain*, a book of Bible verses chosen by her mother Jessie Orton Jones.

1945 ➤ Wins the Caldecott Medal for her illustrations of Rachel Field's book *Prayer for a Child*.

1948 ➤ Golden Books releases Elizabeth's retelling of *Little Red Riding Hood*.

c1953 ➤ Elizabeth begins working on a series of murals at Crotched Mountain Rehabilitation Center in Greenfield, New Hampshire. She becomes caught up in working directly with the children, and never quite finishes the murals. She volunteers at Crotched Mountain for the next 50 years.

1971 ➤ Helps establish *Andy's Playhouse*, a children's community theater, in Mason. Elizabeth writes plays and makes costumes until Andy's moves to Wilton in 1985.

c1992 ➤ Purchases a second home in Mason which she names *Rockabye*.

2002 ➤ Elizabeth receives the *Good Samaritan Award* from Pastoral Counseling Services of Manchester, NH for her volunteer work with children.

2005 ➤ May 10, Elizabeth dies in Peterborough, New Hampshire at age 94.

Note: c1953 means around or about 1953.

Learn More about Elizabeth Orton Jones and Her Work

- Jones, Elizabeth Orton. *Twig*. Reissued by Purple House Press, 2002.
- Field, Rachel and Jones, Elizabeth Orton. *Prayer for a Child*. Simon and Schuster Children's Publishing, 2004.
- Jones, Elizabeth Orton. *Little Red Riding Hood*. Simon and Schuster, 1948. Revised by Helmer, N.

Website:

- *Twentieth Century American Children's Literature*: Elizabeth Orton Jones. Created for University of Oregon Libraries: http://libweb.uoregon.edu/ec/exhibits/childrenslit/eojones.html

Glossary

Caldecott Medal (KAL duh kot MED uhl) An award named in honor of artist Randolph Caldecott. It is given each year to the artist of the most distinguished American picture book for children.

headboard (HED bord) A board or panel at the head of a bed.

pianist (pee AN ist or PEE uh nist) One who plays the piano.

Smithsonian Institution (smith SOH nee uhn IN stuh TOO shuhn) 19 museums and 9 research centers that make up the world's largest museum complex and research organization, located in Washington, D.C.

Crotched Mountain Rehabilitation Center (KROTCH id MOUN tuhn REE uh bil uh tay shuhn SEN tur) A health facility located in Greenfield, NH serving people with disabilities and their families. The campus includes a hospital, school, athletic complex, and wheelchair accessible tree house.

—17—
Ethel Doris "Granny D." Rollins Haddock:
Fighting for a Better America

by Barbara Turner

*N*inety year old Granny D. stood in the People's Hall of the Capitol Rotunda. It was April 21, 2000, just two months after she had finished a 3,200 mile walk across America. She began to give a speech to the gathered crowd about the **First Amendment**. She told how all Americans had the right to free speech and to assemble peacefully. She told how those rights were guaranteed by the **Constitution**.

As she was reading from the Constitution that guaranteed these freedoms, the Capitol Police handcuffed and arrested her. Granny D. was charged with Disorderly Conduct and a trial date was set. At her trial, she was found guilty. The judge, however, believed in what she was doing, and felt she should never have been arrested. He fined her $10.00 and told her to keep up the good work.

· · · · ๑๑ · · · ·

Ethel Doris Rollins was born in Laconia, New Hampshire on January 24, 1910. Her parents called her Doris. In 1927, she went away to Emerson College in Boston, Massachusetts. There, she met Jim Haddock. They married and returned to New Hampshire to raise their family. It wasn't until her children were grown that Doris' life began to change.

The **Atomic Energy Commission** (AEC) had been testing **nuclear** bombs throughout the 1950s. Now they wanted to find "peaceful" uses for their bombs. One idea was to build canals by dropping bombs, but they had to test the idea first. They decided to drop six bombs on Point Hope, Alaska. They told the Inuit villagers that nuclear weapons testing wouldn't harm them. They said the fish the villagers caught after the testing would be safe to eat, too.

The **Inuit** knew these were lies. They looked for help. Doris and her husband heard about the problem. They drove to Alaska and learned about it first hand. When they returned home, they spread the word. They called politicians and scientists. They mailed pamphlets and letters. They told everybody who would listen. The AEC was embarrassed and gave up. The fishing village was saved!

Doris and Jim went back to their normal lives. In 1972, they retired and moved to Dublin, New Hampshire. Jim grew ill with **Alzheimer's Disease** and Doris cared for him until he died. Doris' health began to fail, too. She developed **emphysema** and **arthritis**.

In 1995, two senators saw that big businesses were giving lots of money to politicians. They saw politicians making laws that helped those businesses instead of the American people. They tried to pass a bill (law) to stop this. It failed.

Doris believed in what they were trying to do. She believed politicians should work for the people. She decided to let Americans know what was going on. She would walk across America and tell them.

Doris took on the name of Granny D., and on January 1, 1999, she set out from Pasadena, California, to walk to Washington, DC. She was 88 years old. Her joints ached, and it was hard for her to breathe. Still, she walked ten miles each day, regardless of the weather. She talked to people along the way and told them to make their voices heard. She told them not to let big businesses take over their government.

Doris walked through many states and the **media** followed. They put her on TV and in newspapers. On February 29, 2000, Granny D. reached Washington, DC and was met by a cheering crowd. She was 90 years old and had walked 3,200 miles!

But that wasn't the end for Granny D. In 2004, at age 94, she ran for the US Senate. She lost, but she did get 34% of the vote. In 2007, Granny D. was still traveling and talking to Americans about taking their country back. She said, "We live in a land where each person's voice matters. We can all do something."

TIDBITS

Granny D.'s walk across America took fourteen months. Along the way, she celebrated two birthdays, wore out four pairs of shoes, and cross-country skied for 100 miles of the journey. Her emphysema also improved greatly.

—◆—

At age 90, Granny D. dressed in a mermaid costume at the Weeki Wachee Springs theme park in Tampa, Florida. She also fed the alligators. It was part of a job swap so working women could get out and vote.

Timeline: Granny D. Haddock

1910	➤	January 24, Ethel Doris Rollins is born in Laconia, NH, the second of five children. Her parents call her Doris.
1927	➤	Attends Emerson College in Boston, Massachusetts. Studies to become an actress.
1930	➤	December 31, marries Jim Haddock in a secret ceremony in Boston's Trinity Church.
1931	➤	Is expelled from college for being married.
1933	➤	Daughter Betty is born.
1935	➤	Son Jim is born.
1960	➤	She and her husband save an Inuit fishing village in Point Hope, Alaska, from the "peaceful" use of **nuclear** bombs by the Atomic Energy Commission.
1972	➤	Retires from her job as Production Cost Estimator at a Manchester, NH shoe company. She and her husband move to Dublin, NH.
1992	➤	Husband Jim dies from Alzheimer's Disease.
1999	➤	January 1, begins her walk across America to bring attention to campaign finance reform. Starts in Pasadena, California at the Rose Bowl.
2000	➤	February 29, completes her walk of 3,200 miles at the capitol, Washington, DC. Is awarded an honorary degree from Emerson College.
2001	➤	She and Dennis Burke write *Granny D.: Walking Across America in My Ninetieth Year*.
2002	➤	October 21, is awarded an honorary degree from Franklin Pierce College.
2004	➤	August 19th, officially changes her middle name to 'Granny D.' Runs for the NH Senate as a Democrat against Republican Judd Gregg. Documentary film *Run, Granny Run*, is made.
2007	➤	September, gives speech at the annual Fighting Bob Festival in Wisconsin The Fighting Bob Fest is held each fall. Speakers discuss important national issues.

Learn More about Granny D. and Activism

- Lewis, Barbara A., Espeland, Pamela, and Pernu, Caryn, *The Kid's Guide to Social Activism: How to Solve the Social Problems You Choose – And Turn Creative Thinking into Positive Action*. Free Spirit Publishing, Revised Edition, 1988.

- Breskin Zalben, Jane, *Paths to Peace: People Who Changed the World*. Dutton, 2006.

- Soto, Gary, *Cesar Chavez: A Hero for Everyone*. Aladdin, 2003.

Websites:

- Granny D.'s homepage:
  http://www.grannyd.com

- Weekly Reader Article on 10 Year old Lily Thorpe who started Kids Campaign, a political group for kids to bring better education to Colorado schools:
  http://www.eduplace.com/kids/socsci/fl/books/bke/wklyrdr/u5_article2.shtml

Glossary

Alzheimer's Disease (ALLTS hi muhrz) A serious disease of the brain that causes memory loss and other problems.

arthritis (ar THRYE tiss) A disease that makes a person's joints painful and swollen.

Atomic Energy Commission [AEC] (uh TOM ik en UR jee kuh MISH UHN) A government agency that managed the building, use, and control of nuclear energy by both the military and civilians. The AEC no longer exists. It was replaced by the U.S. Nuclear Regulatory Commission.

constitution (KON stuh TOO shuhn) The system of laws in a country that state the rights of the people and the powers of the government.

emphysema (em fi SEE muh) A disease of the lungs that causes difficulty in breathing.

First Amendment (FURST uh MEND muhnt) The first of 10 changes made to the U.S. Constitution, called the Bill of Rights. The First Amendment guarantees citizens freedom of speech, religion, the right to assemble peacefully among other things

Inuit (IN oo it or IN yoo it) The people from the Arctic north of Canada, Alaska and Greenland, also called Eskimos.

media (MEE dee uh) Ways of communicating information to large numbers of people such as television, radio, or the Internet.

nuclear (NOO klee ur) Having to do with energy created by splitting atoms.

radiation (ray dee AY shuhn) A harmful substance sent off from atoms when they are split.

May Sidore Gruber:
Knitting the Pandora Empire

by Janet Buell

May Sidore had just buried her husband of 36 years. Saul had died suddenly a few days earlier. May was still reeling from the shock of his loss. Now, she had to make a decision. May and her family owned a Manchester, New Hampshire knitting company called Pandora. Saul also owned part of it. Before Saul died, she, Saul, and her parents had disagreements about who would control the company. May wanted to run Pandora. She would need to raise enough money to buy out the other family members. Would she be able to raise the cash she needed?

· · · · ⌒ · · · ·

May Blum was born into the world of New York City knitting. Her mother and father owned a company that made sweaters on big knitting machines. The company eventually became Pandora. Pandora made fashionable sweaters that were sold all over the world. The family faced years of good **profits** and poor ones in the tough fashion industry.

1933 was the era of the drummer. These traveling salesmen drummed up business. They went from town to town opening their sample cases to store buyers. May was only 21 when she took on the job of drummer. That was young for a woman in a job that was done mostly by men. She went **on the road** anyway. Saul and May mapped out her route, and Boston was the first stop. The big department store Macy's was the first to give May an order for sweaters.

May also entered a contest to get into a special business school. Several hundred people competed for only twenty openings. May was one of the twenty picked. Good math skills and a spunky attitude helped her get in.

May, Saul, and her family moved the business to New Hampshire in 1940. As the business grew, May took time out to be a mom to her five children. She also started Manchester's first League of Women Voters. She published a newsletter called *Voice of the Voter*.

May had a passion for writing. *The Yarn* was her newspaper for Pandora employees. She and Saul also started a weekly **subscription** newspaper called *The Manchester Free Press*. May drove to Boston for **journalism** classes. She wrote dozens of articles for the newspaper.

Later in her life, May wrote two books. One is an **autobiography** about her life in the knitting business. The other is an advice book on how to plan for a **career** in *any* business.

May did raise over one million dollars to buy out her family. The money came from friends. It came from the **vendors** who

TIDBITS

The name "Pandora" comes from a Greek myth about the world's first woman. Pandora means "all gifts."

trusted May would keep the business up and running. Money came from everywhere. Her secretary even donated $10,000 to May's cause.

May became president of Pandora. Through her hard work, Pandora employed 1,200 workers at its peak. The factory sold more than $30 million of clothing each year.

Love soon found May again. She met and married Samuel Gruber in 1967.

May Sidore Gruber had many careers over her lifetime. She was a wife and mother. She was a partner in a knitting business. At age 52, she became president of Pandora Industries. She sold her first book at 72. May sold the Pandora sweater making business in 1983. She kept the mill buildings that once housed Pandora. May then ran a real estate company to manage the buildings.

Pandora Factory Workers

Pandora Sweater Label

Timeline: May Sidore Gruber

1912	➤	March 6, May Blum is born in New York City.
1931	➤	October 11, May marries Saul O Sidore.
1936	➤	May 14, Sara Mae, the first of May and Saul's five children, is born.
1938	➤	June 24, son Gene is born.
1940	➤	September, May, Saul, and her family move Pandora to Manchester, NH.
1944	➤	September 14, son Ralph is born.
1947	➤	June 13, daughter Rebecca is born.
1949	➤	August 18, daughter Micala is born.
1960	➤	January, May and Saul attend President John F. Kennedy's Inauguration. The idea for the *Manchester Free Press* is born.
		March, The first issue of *The Manchester Free Press* hits the newsstands.
1964	➤	January 4, Saul Sidore dies.
1964–1967	➤	May learns how to become Pandora's president.
1967	➤	October 18, May marries businessman, artist, and musician, Samuel Gruber.
1968	➤	Saul and May's five children start the Saul O Sidore Memorial Foundation, which carries on May and Saul's interests in a strong community.
1983	➤	May sells Pandora Industries to Gulf and Western.
1984	➤	May's first book *Pandora's Pride* is published.
1989	➤	May's second book *Sky Hooks and Track Shoes* is published.

Learn More about May Sidore Gruber

- Gruber, May. *Pandora's Pride*. Lyle Stuart, Inc. 1984.
- Gruber, May. *Sky Hooks and Track Shoes: Climbing Your Career Ladder*. Brick House Publishing Company, 1989.

Websites:

- May Gruber tells about her mother and the Triangle Waist Factory fire in New York City:
  http://www.nhpr.org/node/13564

Glossary

autobiography (aw toh bye OG ruh fee) A book in which the author tells the story of his or her life.

career (kuh RIHR) The work or the series of jobs a person has.

journalism (JUR nuhl iz uhm) The work of gathering and reporting news for newspapers, magazines, and other media.

on the road (on thuh rohd) Traveling from place to place.

profits (PROF itss) The amount of money left after all the costs of running a business have been subtracted from the money earned.

subscription (suhb SKRIP shuhn) An amount of money paid for the regular delivery of a newspaper, magazine or cable TV service.

vendors (VEN durz) People who sell something.

— 19 —
Annalee Thorndike:
Doll Maker and Businesswoman

by Kathleen W. Deady

$\mathcal{A}$nnalee wondered what she and her husband would do. Their farm was failing, and they could no longer earn enough money to pay their bills. But what else could they do to for work?

Annalee thought about the dolls she made. She had sold them before to make money. She could return to making dolls again, but could she sell enough? Could she possibly even build her doll making into a real business?

· · · · ৩ · · · ·

Barbara Annalee Davis was born in Concord, New Hampshire in 1915. As a child, Annalee loved to watch her mother sew. She also loved dolls, but did not play house with them. Instead, she and her mother made doll clothes together as a hobby.

TIDBITS

Annalee's first dolls were **marionettes**.

In the beginning, Annalee's friends were more interested in her dolls than she was. They kept placing orders and giving her ideas for new dolls.

After high school, Annalee began designing dolls and doll clothing. She sold them through the **New Hampshire League of Arts and Crafts** and other places. Annalee wanted to "cough up some money to help out at home."

Annalee made her dolls for display rather than as toys. They were in set positions and had clothes that were sewn on. Anna carefully dyed the **fabric** and hand painted the faces. She created a story to go with each doll.

In 1941, Annalee married Charles "Chip" Thorndike. They settled in Meredith, New Hampshire. Chip started a poultry farm. Annalee helped Chip in the business.

By the early 1950s, their farm failed. Annalee started making dolls again. Chip worked for a knitting company. Before long, he left his job to work with Annalee and help her build her doll making business.

In the beginning, Annalee made the dolls in their kitchen. She hired a few local people to help. They turned their chicken coop into a design room. Chip invented a flexible wire frame for the dolls so that they could be posed. This frame gave the dolls "**mobilitee**." Soon, there were dolls in every room in their house.

Annalee created her dolls based on things her sons liked, such as skiing and swimming. Chip made little wooden parts for the dolls like skis and ski poles. Annalee made faces with different expressions for each line of dolls.

In 1955, her business became Annalee Mobilitee Dolls. The state of New Hampshire asked her to make dolls that were skiing, hunting, and fishing. The dolls helped promote **tourism** in the state. They became very popular.

By 1960, the company was a major business in the area. It sold dolls in forty states, Canada, and Puerto Rico. In 1964, Annalee built her first factory building. She moved the business out of the house.

Annalee continued to add new lines of dolls. Each new line had a theme such as a holiday, event, or profession. The dolls were usually animals such as rabbits, bears, or mice.

Annalee's company grew year after year. She received many awards. People from around the country loved to collect the dolls. Annalee became one of the top doll makers in the country.

What made Annalee's dolls so successful? Why do people want to collect them? Annalee believed it was because they have personality. "It's the positive-ness of the face," she said. "It's the smile. If you smile, someone else has got to smile back."

Annalee Thorndike turned a childhood hobby into a successful business. She died in 2002. Her son Charles continues to run the business. Every year, the company creates new dolls. The dolls still sell throughout the world.

TIDBITS

By the 1980s, Annalee started working more on holiday themes, including Halloween and Thanksgiving.

◂▪▸

Annalee's dolls have clothing and hairstyles from the time period in which they were made.

◂▪▸

Annalee's dolls have been displayed at the White House.

Timeline: Annalee Thorndike

1915 ➤ May 1, Born Barbara Annalee Davis in Concord, New Hampshire, to Emerson and Doris (Ladd) Davis. Oldest of three girls.

1920s ➤ As a child, makes doll clothes with her mother as a hobby.

1933 ➤ Graduates from Concord High School, Concord, New Hampshire. Sells first dolls through New Hampshire League of Arts and Crafts and other small shops.

1941 ➤ April 19, marries Charles "Chip" Thorndike, settles in Meredith, New Hampshire, helps Chip on poultry farm selling eggs and car parts.

1945 ➤ March 17, son Charles "Chuck" Thorndike born.

1947 ➤ November 18, son Townsend "Town" Thorndike born.

Early 1950s ➤ Poultry business fails, Annalee and Chip decide to start doll business.

1954 ➤ Names business *Annalee Mobilitee Dolls*. Farm becomes known as the Factory in the Woods.

1964 ➤ Builds the Parkersburg, the first factory building. Moves business out of house.

1971 ➤ Opens Annalee's Workshop, now the Outlet Store, in Meredith, New Hampshire.

1972 ➤ Publishes first full color catalog.

1974 ➤ Honored as New Hampshire Small Business of the year. First woman business owner to receive award in state.

1983 ➤ Establishes Annalee Doll Museum to display the history of the dolls. Creates Annalee Doll Society for collectors which today has thousands of members.

1997 ➤ The doll company is named "Employer of the Year" for the State of New Hampshire.

Annalee is awarded the Collectibles and Gift Industry Pioneer Award.

Annalee Retires from Company.

2000 ➤ Annalee comes out of retirement to design dolls for collectors.

2002 ➤ April 7, Annalee dies in her home after a short illness at age 87.

Learn More about Annalee, Mobilitee Dolls, and Doll Making

- Mahren, Sue. *Make Your Own Teddy Bears & Bear Clothes*, Williamson Publishing Co., 2000.

- McGraw, Sheila. *Dolls Kids Can Make*. Firefly Books, 1995.

Websites:

- Information about doll makers and their history:
  http://www.anythinggoesinc.net/doll-makers.shtml

- Official site of Annalee Mobilitee Dolls:
  http://www.annalee.com/

- The Story of Annalee Thorndike:
  http://www.annalee.com/ourstory.asp

- "The Dolls of Annalee" from New Hampshire Historical Association Website:
  http://www.nhhistory.org/annaleeexhibit.html

- Information about the history of dolls:
  http://ctdollartists.com/history.htm#Whatisdoll

Glossary

fabric (FAB rik) Cloth, such as felt or wool.

marionettes (ma ree uh NETSS) Puppets that are moved by pulling strings or wires attached to various parts of their bodies.

Mobilitee (moh BIL i tee) A variation on the spelling of the word mobility, meaning moveable, able to be moved. The dolls could be moved and placed in different positions.

New Hampshire League of Arts and Crafts (noo HAMP shur LEEG uv ARTSS and KRAFTSS) An organization that helps people sell their creative work. Today it is called the League of New Hampshire Craftsmen.

tourism (TOOR izm) The business or industry that provides services to people who travel.

Penny Pitou: She Keeps Going and Going and...

by Barbara Turner

*T*ommy stood on the slope and stared down the hill. The wind was cold and stung his face, but he didn't care. He just wanted to ski. He pushed off and sped down hill, going faster and faster until . . . .

SMASH!

Tommy crashed. His hat flew off and a mass of long, blonde hair fell over his shoulders.

The opposing team stared. Tommy was . . . a girl?

· · · · ⚬ · · · ·

"Tommy" was really Penny Pitou. She was born in Bayside, New York on October 8, 1938. When she was three, her parents moved to Center Harbor, New Hampshire. Penny started skiing at age four, and right from the start, it was clear she had talent. She went from skiing on a hill in her backyard to skiing on Belknap Mountain.

In high school, Penny joined the ski team disguised as 'Tommy." In 1953, girls weren't allowed on the Laconia High School team. She was told it was because there were no chaperones on the bus that took them to competitions. Penny's teammates knew who she really was, and they kept her secret. Penny remained on the team, winning competitions for her school, until the day she crashed.

Penny still kept skiing. Her neighbor, Gary Allen, coached her. He talked to famous skiers and asked them questions. What kind of wax did they use? And under what conditions? How long were their skis? Later, he and Penny talked about what he had learned. At 17, Penny won the **Junior Nationals**, coming in first in the **Downhill**, **Slalom** and **Combined**.

Now the Olympics were coming up. Tryouts were being held in Stowe, Vermont. Penny's mom told her to go. Penny didn't want to. Besides being a good skier, Penny was also a good student, and she had already missed a lot of school. Penny's mom continued to encourage her, and finally, Penny went. She tried out and made the 1956 Olympic team.

Penny went to Italy to compete, but did not do well. Andrea Mead Lawrence, a medalist in the 1952 Olympics, told her not to give up. She encouraged Penny to work even harder. Penny did, and in 1960, she made the Olympic team again.

Penny's first race at Squaw Valley, California, was the Women's Downhill. She skied all out and finished with a time of 1:38.6 seconds. It was a very good run. Penny won the Silver medal, just one second behind Germany's Heidi Biebel who took the Gold.

The next day, Penny competed in the Women's Slalom. She swished through the course and finished with a time of 1:40. Another good run, and another Silver medal! This time, she was only one tenth of a second behind the leader, Swiss skier Yvonne Ruegg. It was less time than it took to blink an eye.

Penny went home happy. She had won two Silver medals, and she was the first American–male or female–to medal in Downhill skiing. She had also met a very handsome Austrian skier whom she would later marry.

Today, Penny owns a travel agency in New Hampshire. She plans skiing and hiking trips, and other vacations for her customers. And she still skis. She also believes in giving back to her community. Along with her second husband, Milo Pike, Penny donated $1,000,000 to the New Hampshire Charitable Fund which helps people all across the state.

Penny believes anyone can be successful at anything. "Everyone falls flat on their face sometime," she said. "The trick is to get up and keep going."

Timeline: Penny Pitou

1938	➤	October 8, Penelope 'Penny' Pitou is born in Bayside, New York to Lee and Gus Pitou.
1941	➤	Moves to Center Harbor, New Hampshire.
1955	➤	Wins first place in the Downhill, Slalom and Combined at the Junior Nationals in Whitefish, Montana.
1956	➤	Is US Olympic Ski Team Member in Cortina Italy, competing in all three events.
		Receives Andrea Mead Lawrence Award as "American Junior Skier of the Year."
1959	➤	February 25, Governor Wesley Powell declares it 'Penny Pitou Day' in New Hampshire.
1960	➤	Competes in Olympics at Squaw Valley, California. Wins Silver medal in Downhill and Giant Slalom. Is first American to medal in the Downhill.
		February, appears on the cover of Life Magazine.
1961	➤	Elected to National Ski Hall of Fame as 'best Alpine skier of the year.'
		Marries Egon Zimmerman, Austrian Olympic Team member. They open Penny Pitou Ski School at Gunstock Ski Area in Gilford, NH.
1962	➤	Gives birth to son Christian.
1963	➤	Opens Penny Pitou Ski School in Blue Hills Ski Area in Milton, MA.
1965	➤	Gives birth to son Kim.
		Is named 'Woman of the Year' by *Mademoiselle Magazine*
1968	➤	Marriage to Egon Zimmerman ends.
1974	➤	Buys Lakes Travel Agency in Laconia, NH and renames it Penny Pitou Travel, Inc.
1976	➤	Is elected into National Ski Hall of Fame.
		Is head of Presidential Delegation to Innsbruck, Austria Olympics.
1979	➤	Opens second branch of Penny Pitou Travel, Inc. in Concord, NH.
1981	➤	Marries Milo Pike of Pike Industries.
1996	➤	Opens third branch of Penny Pitou Travel in North Conway, NH.
2001	➤	Inducted into New England Women's Sports Hall of Fame.

Learn More about Skiing and the Winter Olympics

- Crossingham, John, and Kalman, Bobbie. *Skiing In Action*. Crabtree Publishing Co., 2004.
- Brimner, Larry Dane. *Skiing*, Children's Press, 1997.
- Brimner, Larry Dane. *The Winter Olympics*, Children's Press, 1997.

Websites:

- NH Junior Skiing–Site for junior skiers, reviews, classes, equipment, virtual skiing, games:
  http://sakharov.net/skiing/

- Official Olympic Skiing site, history, how to, disciplines:
  http://www.olympic.org/uk/sports/programme/index_uk.asp?SportCode = SI

Glossary

bindings (BINE dingz) The metal locks that attach the ski to the ski boot.

combined (kuhm BINED) An event that includes one downhill run and two slalom runs on a single day.

downhill (DOUN hil) A sport involving sliding down snow-covered hills with a long, thin ski attached to each foot.

Foreign Service (FOR uhn SUR viss) A nation's diplomatic staff (representatives) based in another country.

Junior Nationals (JOO nyer NASH uh nuhlz) A skiing competition for athletes between the ages of 16 and 20.

slalom (SLAH luhm) An athletic event in which competitors ski down a hill, zigzagging between gates (poles).

staves (stayvz) Long thin strips of wood that form the sides of a barrel.

—21—
Jeanne Shaheen: NH's First Elected Woman Governor

by Janet Buell

*J*eanne Shaheen stood outside the New Hampshire State House. Her hand rested on the Bible as she took the oath of office. Family, friends, and others looked on as Jeanne stepped into history – of the United States *and* of New Hampshire. Since 1776, our country has had over 2,400 male governors. Jeanne had just become the 15th woman to hold the job. She was now the *first* woman to be elected governor of New Hampshire.

· · · · ໐ჿ · · · ·

In 1971, Jeanne Shaheen was teaching high school in Mississippi. She heard the words of the newly elected governor of Georgia. Jimmy Carter believed in a more open and honest government. Jeanne liked what Carter had to say.

Later, Jeanne moved to New Hampshire to live with her husband, Billy. She still remembered Jimmy Carter. The former governor of Georgia was now running for president. Jeanne and Billy volunteered to run his

In Mississippi Jeanne taught English to black students who were going to be integrated into all white schools.

◆—◆—

Jeanne credits her parents for inspiring her to be active in politics. When she was young, the whole family watched the news each night. Her parents discussed what was happening in the world. Her father quizzed the girls on current events.

NH presidential campaign. It was a race no one thought Carter could win. He eventually *did* win the support of New Hampshire's citizens. From there, Carter went on to win the presidency. People credited Jeanne and Billy for his success with New Hampshire voters.

Jeanne discovered she was good at organizing other people's campaigns. Several politicians asked her to help them run their campaigns. Newspaper reports called her a smart political planner. During this time, Jeanne and Billy were also raising their three daughters.

Jeanne decided to run for New Hampshire state senate in 1990. She won the senate race and went on to be reelected twice.

By this time, Jeanne was ready for bigger things. In 1996, she ran for governor, and won.

Jeanne entered the governor's office with strong goals. They included helping young people by building New Hampshire's education system. Her other goals were to help the environment, businesses, **civil rights**, and health care. Jeanne signed the law making a day to honor Martin Luther King, Jr. New Hampshire was the last state to honor King in this way.

While she was governor, Jeanne ran for the United States Senate and lost to John Sununu. When Al Gore ran against George Bush in 2002, Jeanne was on his **short list** of Vice Presidential candidates. Jeanne said she didn't want to run for vice president at that time.

In 2003, she took over as National Campaign Chair of John Kerry's campaign. Again, people credited her with helping Kerry. He went on to win the Democratic nomination for president.

In 2005, Harvard University offered Jeanne a job as director of the Institute of Politics and the Kennedy School of Government.

At the Kennedy School, Jeanne worked with young people interested in **public service**. Her work with young women was especially important. Jeanne felt strongly that more young women should be elected to public office. Today, only 28 women have been governors of the states.

In 2007, Jeanne announced she was running for the United States Senate. Only time will tell if Jeanne Shaheen will make history again by being the first woman from New Hampshire elected to the United States Senate.

TIDBITS

Jeanne served on the student council and also was elected to political office in college.

Vesta Roy was the first female governor of New Hampshire, but she was not elected to the position. She was appointed when Governor Hugh Gallen died. Roy served for seven days until governor-elect, John Sununu, took office.

Jeanne at the unveiling of her official portrait.

Timeline: Jeanne Shaheen

1947 ➤ January 28, Jeanne is born to Ivan and Belle Bowers in St. Charles, Missouri. She is the second of three daughters.

1964 through 1969 ➤ Jeanne attends Shippensburg University in Shippensburg, PA, where she receives a Bachelor of Arts degree in English

1973 ➤ Jeanne receives a **Master's Degree** in **Political Science** from the University of Mississippi.

1973 ➤ Jeanne **elopes** with Billy Shaheen.

1973 ➤ Jeanne moves to New Hampshire. Here, she teaches public speaking at Dover High School. She and Billy run a small leather and silver business at York Beach, Maine.

1974 ➤ September, Stefany, the first of Jeanne and Bill's three daughters, is born.

1978 ➤ January, daughter Stacey is born.

1980 ➤ Jeanne runs Jimmy Carter's NH campaign for president.

1985 ➤ December, third daughter, Molly, is born.

1990 ➤ Jeanne becomes a candidate for the New Hampshire state senate. She beats the **incumbent** and goes on to serve for three terms.

1996 ➤ Jeanne is elected governor of New Hampshire.

1998 ➤ Jeanne is re-elected governor of NH.

1999 ➤ Jeanne signs a law making Martin Luther King, Jr.'s birthday a state holiday.

2000 ➤ Jeanne is elected to a third term as governor. Only three other NH governors had been elected to three terms.

2000 & 2001 ➤ Jeanne is chosen to serve as Chair of the Education Commission of the States.

2002 ➤ Jeanne runs against John Sununu for the US Senate. She is narrowly defeated.

2003–2004 ➤ Jeanne manages John Kerry's political campaign for president.

2005 ➤ July 1, Jeanne becomes the Director of Harvard University's Institute of Politics.

2007 ➤ September, Jeanne Shaheen announces her **candidacy** for United States Senate.

Learn More about Governors and Women in Politics

- De Capua, Sarah. *Being a Governor*. Children's Press, 2004.
- Degezelle, Terri and Ponomareff, Shirley Tabata. *Voting in Elections*. First Facts Books, 2005.
- Hamilton, John. *Voting in an Election*. Checkerboard Books, 2004.
- Monroe, Judy. *The Susan B. Anthony's Voting Rights Trial*. Enslow Publishers, 2002.

Websites:

- Center for American Women and Politics: http://www.cawp.rutgers.edu/index.html
- For women's political firsts: http://www.cawp.rutgers.edu/Facts/firsts.html
- To learn how young women can become more involved, go to The White House Project: http://thewhitehouseproject.org/voterunlead/golead/18ways.php
- The Younger Women's Task Force: http://www.ywtf.org/ywtf/home.aspx

Glossary

candidacy (KAN di duh see) A person's run for political office.

civil rights (SIV il RITESS) The rights that all members of a society have to freedom and equal treatment under the law.

elope (i LOPE) To run away to get married without letting anyone else know.

incumbent (in KUHM bent) A person elected to an political office.

master's degree (MASS turz di GREE) A college degree that is earned after at least one additional year of study beyond four years of college.

political science (poh LIT I kul sye uhnss) The study of government and how it works.

public service (PUHB lik SUR viss) Acts performed for the good of the community.

short list (SHORT list) In politics, a list of possible nominees.

— 22 —
Christa McAuliffe:
Teacher in Space

by Kathleen W. Deady

Christa McAuliffe stood in the Roosevelt Room at the White House. It was July 19, 1985. With her were nine other teachers from across the country. One had been picked to fly into space. That one would teach people about space travel from on board the **Space Shuttle** Challenger.

The teachers looked out at the huge crowd of reporters, photographers, and cameras. They listened as Vice President George H. W. Bush spoke to the country. "We are here today to announce the first **private citizen** in the history of space flight," he said. "And the winner. . .is Christa McAuliffe."

Christa could not believe she had been chosen. She always had thought space travel was exciting, and she loved to teach. For Christa, teaching from space would be a dream come true.

· · · · ⌒ · · · ·

Sharon Christa Corrigan was born in Boston, Massachusetts in 1948. Growing up, she saw the beginnings of the space program. Space travel excited Christa. She said to a friend. "Do you realize that some day people will be going to the moon . . . I want to do that."

Christa was a good student and liked to learn. In high school, she played basketball and softball. She took piano lessons and performed in musical plays. She also met Steve McAuliffe. In 1970, Christa graduated from Framingham State College. That summer, Christa married Steve.

Christa and Steve moved to Washington, DC. Christa taught school while Steve attended law school. In 1976, their son Scott was born. Two years later, the family moved to Concord, New Hampshire. The next year, they had a daughter, Caroline.

Christa continued teaching. Her students loved her because she made her lessons exciting. She believed hands-on experiences were the best way for students to learn. Christa was often called the Field Trip Teacher.

By 1984, space flights were common. President Reagan wanted to excite people about space travel again. He said he would send a regular person into space. That person would be a teacher.

Christa applied to the Teacher in Space Program. She had to write about a project she would do in space. For her project, Christa decided she would keep a journal of her experience. She also had to explain why she wanted to go. Christa wrote, "I watched the Space Age being born and I would like to participate." After 5 months, **NASA** picked Christa.

Christa trained with NASA for 6 months. She learned all about the shuttle and the equipment. She experienced the feeling of being weightless. She learned how to eat, dress, and

TIDBITS

Christa developed a course called *The American Woman*, which she taught in Concord High School. The course is still being taught today.

The application to be the Teacher in Space was 25 pages long and took many hours to complete. Christa did not mail hers in until the last day possible.

Christa was one of over 11,000 teachers to apply for the Teacher in Space program.

Christa did not think she would be picked. Some of the teachers were doctors, authors, and scholars.

•◆•

Christa could not wait to teach about space travel from Space. She called the trip she would be going on the **Ultimate** Field Trip.

use the bathroom in space. Christa even learned how to sleep while floating in the shuttle.

On January 28, 1986, people watched the launch on television. They saw the Challenger head into space. Christa and six other astronauts were on board. It was a very cold morning. The cold had damaged part of the spacecraft. The Challenger exploded 73 seconds after lift-off. The explosion killed everyone on board.

The country was shocked and very sad. People held **memorial** services. They found many ways to remember Christa and the rest of the crew.

In 1990, the Christa McAuliffe **Planetarium** opened in Concord, New Hampshire. People from around the country go there to learn about space. They go to remember Christa. And they go to learn about her dream and to help keep it alive.

Christa learns about working under weightless conditions.

Timeline: Christa McAuliffe

1948 ➤ September 2, born Sharon Christa Corrigan to Edward and Grace Corrigan, oldest of five children.

1954 ➤ Family moves to Framingham, Mass.

1958 ➤ President Eisenhower starts NASA, the National Aeronautics and Space Administration.

1961 ➤ NASA begins testing manned space flights.
May 5, Christa sees Alan Shepard become first American to travel into space.

1962 ➤ February 20, John Glenn **orbits** the earth three times and lands safely in the Atlantic Ocean.

1962–1966 ➤ Attends Marion High School in Framingham, MA.
Meets Steven McAuliffe in sophomore year.

1970 ➤ Graduates from Framingham State College with degree in History.
August 23, marries Steve McAuliffe. They move to Maryland.

1970–1978 ➤ Teaches in Maryland.

1976 ➤ September 11, son Scott born.

1978 ➤ Earns Masters degree in School Administration from Bowie State College, Bowie, Maryland. Moves soon afterward to Concord, New Hampshire.

1978–1979 ➤ Teaches at Rundlett Junior High School in Concord, New Hampshire.

1979 ➤ August 24, daughter Caroline born.

1980–1982 ➤ Teaches at Bow Memorial (Middle) School in Bow, New Hampshire.

1982–1985 ➤ Teaches at Concord High School in Concord, New Hampshire.

1985 ➤ February 1, Applies to Teacher in Space program.
July 19, Chosen from over 11,500 applicants.

1985 ➤ September, begins training at NASA facility in Houston, Texas.

1986 ➤ January 28, dies along with six other astronauts in explosion of Space Shuttle Challenger in Florida.

1990 ➤ Christa McAuliffe Planetarium opens in Concord, New Hampshire.

Learn More About Christa McAuliffe and Space Travel

- Billings, Charlene. ***Christa McAuliffe, Pioneer Space Teacher.*** Enslow Publishers, Inc., 1986.
- Naden, Corinne J. ***Christa McAuliffe, Teacher in Space.*** Millbrook Press, 1991.
- Jaffrey, Laura S. ***Christa McAuliffe, A Space Biography.*** Enslow Publishers, Inc. 1998.

Websites:

- Information on Christa McAuliffe and the Christa McAuliffe Planetarium:
  http://www.starhop.com/cm_bio.htm
- NASA's page for Kids:
  http://www.nasa.gov/audience/forkids/home/index.html
- Biographical Data on Christa McAuliffe, Lyndon B. Johnson Space Center Website:
  http://www.jsc.nasa.gov/Bios/htmlbios/mcauliffe.html

Glossary

memorial (muh MOR ee uhl) Something planned or made to help remember a person or event, such as a service, a monument, a building, or a holiday.

NASA (NA saw) (**National Aeronautics and Space Administration**) An agency started in 1958 by President Dwight Eisenhower to study and explore space.

orbit (OR bit) To move or travel around a planet, the sun, etc.

planetarium (PLAN uh TAIR ee uhm) A building that uses projectors to make images that represent the solar system and has seats for an audience.

private citizen (PRYE vit SIT i zuhn) A person who does not hold a public or government office or job.

space shuttle (SPAYSS SHUHT uhl) A spacecraft designed to carry astronauts into space and back to earth.

ultimate (UHL tuh mit) Last or final; greatest or best.

Linda Stewart Dalianis: NH's First Woman Supreme Court Justice

by M. Lu Major

*T*he courthouse guard watched the dark-haired woman drive her car into the parking lot. She pulled into a space reserved for judges. The guard rushed over to stop her. He tried to be polite but he knew his job.

"I'm sorry, dearie," he said to the woman, "but you can't park here."

Linda Dalianis smiled at the guard. "That's *Judge Dearie*," she said.

Judge Dalianis was not angry at the man. She understood the reason for his mistake. The guard did not yet know who she was. She was the first woman named to be a judge in New Hampshire's Superior Court.

· · · · ᕲᕤ · · · ·

Linda Stewart was born in 1948 in Boston, Massachusetts. Later, her family moved to Framingham. Linda grew up loving animals. At first, she dreamed of becoming a veterinarian. Linda was told women could not become animal doctors. She was only a child and believed this statement. Linda was very disappointed. She decided she would have to find a different career.

When Linda was around 12, her family moved to New Hampshire. After high school, Linda attended Northeastern University. At first, Linda thought she might want to write for newspapers. Later she decided to go to law school. She graduated from Northeastern University and entered Suffolk University Law School. She received her law degree in 1974.

Linda worked for a Nashua, New Hampshire law firm for several years. In 1979 the Superior Court made her the first female marital master. A marital master is a lawyer who makes decisions about divorce cases. They help the families decide about **child support** payments and **custody** of the children.

In 1980, Linda was appointed by Governor Hugh Gallen to be the first woman justice of the Superior Court. Some state officials questioned the governor's choice. Linda was expecting a baby. They wondered if a pregnant woman could do the job. But Linda proved them wrong. She did not believe becoming a judge should be limited only to men. "I was aware that I had to work harder...in order to be regarded as an equal," Linda said. Soon it did not matter that a woman had been given the job.

The Superior Court hears more difficult cases, such as crimes. Superior Court judges often stay on the job until they retire at age 70. Linda Dalianis worked for nearly 20 years in the Superior Court system.

In March, 2000, Governor Jeanne Shaheen named Judge Dalianis the first woman Chief Justice of New Hampshire Superior Court. The Chief Justice hears cases but she also manages the court's business. She is in charge of all the people who work there.

The following month, New Hampshire's highest **judicial** body, the Supreme Court, had an opening. The Supreme Court is the last place a person can **appeal** a **verdict** in his or her own state. Governor Shaheen decided to name a woman to the state's highest court. She nominated Chief Justice Dalianis. When she took her oath of office, Justice Dalianis said, "I look forward to a **legacy** that will live long into the future . . ." Today her title is Senior Associate Justice of the Supreme Court.

Justice Dalianis believes in the American court system. She spends many hours at her job reviewing cases. She also spends time teaching others about the courts. In 2001 she traveled to Vologda, Russia. There, she helped Russian judges develop ways to train other judges. The work was long and hard. Every word had to go through Russian interpreters.

Justice Dalianis also visits local schools. She and other members of the Supreme Court explain their jobs to students. It is a job she loves and takes seriously. A lawyer once said of Justice Dalianis, "People have trust in her fairness. . ."

TIDBITS

New Hampshire was nearly the last state to put a woman on its Supreme Court. Only South Dakota was left to nominate a woman to its highest court.

Members of the NH Supreme Court. Left to Right: Justice Richard Galway, Justice Linda Dalianis, Justice John Broderick

Timeline: Linda Stewart Dalianis

1948	➤	Linda is born in Boston, Massachusetts to John and Irene Stewart.
1954	➤	The Stewart family moves to Framingham, Massachusetts.
1960	➤	The Stewart family moves to Peterborough, NH.
1970	➤	Graduates from Northeastern University, Boston Massachusetts. She graduates *Cum Laude* (Latin for "with honor") with a Bachelor of Arts degree.
1972	➤	Marries Griffin Dalianis.
1974	➤	Earns law degree from Suffolk University Law School. Admitted to the NH state bar.
1976	➤	Gives birth to first son.
1974–1979	➤	Practices law in a private firm in Nashua, NH.
1979	➤	Gives birth to a daughter. The daughter dies in infancy.
1979	➤	First woman lawyer appointed marital master in New Hampshire.
1980	➤	Begins serving as a NH Superior Court judge.
1981	➤	Gives birth to second son.
1982	➤	Receives the Outstanding Alumni Award from Northeastern University.
2000	➤	March, 15th, becomes Chief Justice of the NH Superior Court. April 25, appointed to the New Hampshire Supreme Court by Governor Jeanne Shaheen.
2001	➤	Justice Dalianis travels to Russia to assist the Russian courts with law workshops.
2007	➤	Becomes the Senior **Associate** Justice of the NH Supreme Court.

Learn More about Linda Stewart Dalianis and the Court System

- Dubois, Muriel. *The United States Supreme Court.* Capstone Press, 2004.

- McElroy, Linda Tucker. *Meet My Grandmother: She's a Supreme Court Justice.* Millbrook Press, 2000.

- Weiss, Carrie. *Step Into the Courtroom: An Overview of Laws, Courts, and Jury Trials.* Dandy Lions Books, 2003.

Websites:

- About New Hampshire Courts:
  http://www.nhbar.org
  http://www.courts.state.nh.us/supreme/meetdalian.htm

Glossary

appeal (uh PEEL) A request to take a case to a higher court for review.

associate (uh SOH she it) One who is joined with others in a group or business.

child support (CHILDE suh PORT) An amount of money the law says a divorced parent must pay to provide for a child.

custody (KUHSS tuh dee) The legal right to look after a child.

judicial (joo-DISH-uhl) The branch of the government that explains and applies the law.

justice (JUHSS tiss) Another word for judge. This term is often reserved for judges who serve in the Supreme Court, the highest court in a state our country.

legacy (LEG uh see) Something handed down from generation to generation.

verdict (VUR dikt) the decision by a jury on whether an accused person is guilty or not guilty.

Lynn Jennings:
Distance Runner

by M. Lu Major

Lynn Jennings ran all the way home from Bromfield High School. At least this time, she wasn't last. Running alone, she didn't have to stare at somebody else's back.

Lynn was the only girl on the track team. The Harvard, Massachusetts high school didn't have a girl's team so coach John Babington let Lynn join the boys. Lynn was fast, and she was determined, but she couldn't keep up with the boys. Physically she couldn't match their **stamina** and longer strides. But Lynn wouldn't stop running. It was what she loved to do most in the world.

An average kid would have rested once she reached home. Not Lynn. Running home from school was just one part of her daily **workout**. When she reached the door, she called her Springer Spaniel, Otis. The dog was Lynn's loyal and enthusiastic training partner. The two took off, heading back to Bromfield High and extra practice. Someday, Lynn believed, she would be *first*.

· · · · ୨୬ · · · ·

Lynn Jennings was born in Princeton, New Jersey in 1960. Even as a little girl, she loved to run. She raced around her house and asked her father to time her.

Lynn's family moved several times. She lived in Scotland for a while. She won her first race there when she was six years old. She was always the fastest kid in elementary school.

In high school, Lynn was no longer the fastest. The bigger, stronger boys could always beat her times. Lynn had to think of herself not just as an athlete, but as a female athlete.

She dreamed of being the fastest woman in the world. She wanted to win an Olympic medal. Lynn loved distance running, however. When she was a teenager the Olympic Games did not have a distance competition for women. The longest race was only 1500 meters. Lynn later said, "It was hard for me to believe that I was dreaming about something that didn't really exist."

At 17, Lynn ran in her first Boston Marathon. She ran the 26 mile course in 2 hours and 46 minutes. That time would have given her third place. But her time didn't count. Marathon athletes must be at least 18. Lynn soon learned why. The hard, long miles had damaged her left knee. Surgery corrected the problem.

Lynn attended Princeton University. She joined the women's track team. Lynn focused on distance running. She says her years at Princeton were hard and sometimes frustrating. Lynn was a good student but at first she did not do well on the track team. Finally, during her senior year, Lynn found success. The **frustrations** in college, she once

TIDBITS

After college, Lynn spent three years training without a coach.

•–•–•

John Babington was not only Lynn's high school coach. He later became her coach when she raced professionally.

TIDBITS

Lynn Jennings won 39 national running titles—more than any other man or woman.

said, ". . . pretty much helped me fire up my career as an adult."

Around 1985, Lynn moved to Newmarket, New Hampshire. She found a small cabin at the end of a long, dirt road. Lynn coached herself. Later a professional track club called Athletics West offered Lynn a running **contract**. Soon Lynn was competing in Europe. She set five personal records.

Lynn qualified for the Olympics in 1988. She came in 6th in the 10K (10,000 meter) race. The Nike shoe company became her **sponsor**. Four years later, Lynn won the bronze medal in the 1992 Olympics in the same race.

Lynn Jennings won nine cross-country titles. She won three world championships. After 26 years, she and her husband, David Hill, left New Hampshire. They moved to Portland, Oregon. She retired in 2006. That same year, she was elected to the United States Track and Field Hall of Fame. Today Lynn bikes and is on a rowing team. She still runs for health and pleasure.

1990: Lynn Jennings wins a cross-country championship in France.

Timeline: Lynn Jennings

1960	➤	Born July 1, 1960 in Princeton, New Jersey.
1977	➤	Enters the Boston marathon unofficially and posts a time of 2 hours and 46 minutes.
1978	➤	Graduates from Bromfield School in Harvard, Massachusetts.
1983	➤	Graduates from Princeton University, Princeton, New Jersey with a degree in history.
1984	➤	Participates in her first Olympic trials but came in last in the heats.
1988	➤	Comes in 6th in the 10,000 meter race in the Olympic Games.
1989	➤	November, is the United States cross-country champion in San Francisco.
1990	➤	November, is the U.S. cross-country champion in New York.
		December, is named runner of the year by the women's long-distance running committee of the Athletics Congress.
		December, is voted 10th annual Jesse Owens Award winner as U.S. outstanding performer in track and field.
1991	➤	September 15, marries David Hill.
1992	➤	Bronze medalist in the 1992 Olympic Games for the 10,000 meter race in Barcelona, Spain.
1993	➤	Lynn is the world indoor bronze medalist for the 3000 meter race.
1995	➤	Lynn is the world indoor silver medalist for the 3000 meter race.
1996	➤	Competes in the Olympic Games in Altanta, Georgia.
2000	➤	Lynn moves to Portland, Oregon.
2006	➤	March 22, she officially retires from racing.

Learn More about Lynn Jennings and Running

- Reynolds, Susan. The First Marathon: *The Legend of Pheidippides.* Albert Whitman & Company, 2006.

- Rutledge, Rachel. *Best Of Best/Track & Field (Women of Sports).* Millbrook Press, 1999.

- Wolden Nitz, Kristin. *Play-By-Play Track (Play-By-Play).* Lerner Publications, 2003.

Websites:

Interview with Lynn Jennings:

- www.kidsrunning.com/columns/krcolumnstheyranlynn.html

- www.runningtimes.com/rt/articles/?id = 9490&page = 1

Glossary

contract (KON trakt) A legal agreement between people stating the terms by which one will work for the other.

frustration (fruhss TRAY shun) A feeling of helplessness or discouragement.

sponsor (SPON sur) To pay the costs for someone or something in exchange for having your products advertised by the sponsored person.

stamina (STAM uh nuh) The energy and strength to keep doing something for a long time.

workout (WURK out) Physical exercise; practice for a sport.

— 25 —
Jenny Thompson:
Olympic Swimmer

by Kathleen W. Deady

*J*enny Thompson watched her teammates and waited for her turn to swim. It was July 1992. She had made it to the Olympic Games in Barcelona, Spain. Jenny was the anchor leg, the last of the four swimmers. She did not want to let her team down.

The team was a meter behind as Jenny hit the water. She blocked out the noise and swam the last 100 meters as fast as she could. When she reached the end, she looked up at the scoreboard. Her time of 54.01 seconds was the fastest in history. The team set a new world record. Jenny had won her first Olympic gold medal. It would not be her last.

· · · · ᧕ · · · ·

Jennifer Elizabeth Thompson was born in Danvers, Massachusetts in 1973. Even as a baby, Jenny loved being in water. She would take a deep

TIDBITS

In 1994 Jenny broke her arm at college. Doctors fixed it with a titanium plate and seven screws. Two weeks later, Jenny won the 100 meter freestyle at the U.S. National swim races.

• • •

In Jenny's four years at Stanford University, the women's swim team was undefeated. [They won every single dual meet, conference championship, and NCAA title.]

breath and swim underwater between her mother and her brothers. As her family says, she could swim before she could walk.

Growing up, Jenny swam in nearby pools. She was one of the youngest members on her Dolphin Team at the Danvers YMCA. In her first meet, Jenny swam so fast she set a new district record for the 25-yard **butterfly**. She also took first place in two other races.

In the summer of 1984, Jenny was 11 years old. The Olympics were in Los Angeles, California. Jenny loved watching the U.S. teams and the medal ceremonies. She especially liked the swimmers. She wondered if maybe she would be in the Olympics someday.

This was a hard time for Jenny. She learned she had **scoliosis** and had to wear a back brace. She was also teased in school because she was taller and stronger than others.

When she was twelve, Jenny joined the Seacoast Swimming Association (SSA) in Dover, New Hampshire. Her family moved to Dover to be close to SSA. Jenny **qualified** for the Junior National Swim Competition. She made the finals and took 6th place.

At fourteen, Jenny made the US swim team. She won her first international gold medal at the Pan American Games. She was the youngest U.S. gold medal winner ever.

In 1991, Jenny graduated from Dover High School. She entered Stanford University and joined the swim team. The next spring, she tried out for the Olympics. Only the two fastest swimmers would make the team. Jenny remembered what her coach told her. "Before you do something, you have to believe you can do it." Jenny believed she could set a new world record.

At the opening **trial**, Jenny took first place and did set a new world record. She finished first again in the finals and made the team. At the Olympics in July, Jenny won two gold medals. Both times were new world records. She also won a silver medal.

Jenny continued on the U.S. swim team for several years. She won many awards in the U.S. and around the world. Jenny returned to the Olympics in 1996, 2000, and 2004. She won more Olympic medals than any U.S. swimmer in history.

In 2001, Jenny started medical school. She earned her degree in 2006. Today, Jenny is a doctor and works as an **anesthesiologist**.

2004: Jenny competes in the Olympic Trials in Long Beach, California.

Timeline: Jenny Thompson

1973	February 26, born Jennifer Elizabeth Thompson in Danvers, Massachusetts to Margrid Thompson, youngest of four children.
1981	Joined the Dolphins swim team at the Danvers, Massachusetts YMCA.
c1984	Was diagnosed with scoliosis and forced to wear a back brace.
c1985	Joins the Seacoast Swimming Association in Dover, New Hampshire. Before long, the family moves to Dover so Jenny can be closer to her swimming coach.
	Qualifies for Junior Nationals in Alabama. Takes 6th place.
1987	Won the 50 meter freestyle in the Pan American Games, her first international gold and also takes 3rd place in the 100 meter **freestyle**.
1991	Graduates from Dover High School in Dover, New Hampshire, enters Stanford University as a human biology major and joins the swim team.
	Wins her first World Championship as part of the USA's 4x100 Freestyle Relay Team.
1992	Participates in the Olympics in Barcelona, Spain. Wins a gold medal in the 4x100 **meter medley relay** and a silver in the 100 meter freestyle competitions.
1995	Graduates from Stanford University with a degree in Human Biology.
	Jenny's childhood swimming pool, the Guppey Pool in Dover, New Hampshire, is renamed The Jenny Thompson Competition Pool.
1996	The Olympics are held in Atlanta. Jenny wins gold medals in the 4x100 freestyle relay, the 4x200 meter freestyle relay, and the 4x100 meter medley relay.
1997–1999	Jenny wins eight more world championships.
2000	The Olympics are held in Sydney, Australia. Jenny wins gold medals in the 4 x 200 meter freestyle relay and the 4x100 meter medley relay as well as a bronze medal in the 100 meter freestyle.
2004	February 10, Jenny's mother dies of cancer at age 65.
	At age 31, Jenny is the oldest member of the US. swim team. She becomes only the third female swimmer to qualify for four Olympic Games.
2006	She earns an advanced medical degree from Columbia University's College of Physicians and Surgeons.
2007	She is one of eight athletes inducted into Stanford University's Hall of Fame.

NOTE: c1984 means around or about 1984.

Learn More about Jenny Thompson and Swimming

- Greenber, Doreen and Michael. ***Fast Lane to Victory: The Story of Jenny Thompson***. Wish Publishing, 2001.

Websites:

- Official United States Olympic Team biography of Jenny Thompson: http://www.usoc.org/26_1247.htm

- Jenny Thompson's Awards and Accomplishments: http://sports.jrank.org/pages/4827/Thompson-Jenny.html

Glossary

anesthesiologist (an iss THEE zee AW loh jist) A doctor who specializes in giving people drugs or gas to prevent pain during operations.

butterfly (BUHT ur flye) A swim stroke in which the swimmer moves her arms in a windmill style.

freestyle medley (FREE stile MED lee) A swim event in which the swimmers can swim in any style.

medley relay (MED lee REE lay) A swim event in which the swimmers can swim any style except the backstroke, breaststroke, or butterfly.

meter (MEE tur) The basic unit of length in the metric system. A meter is equal to 39.37 inches or 3 1/4 feet.

qualify (KWAHL uh fye) To reach a level or standard that allows you to do something.

scoliosis (skoh lee OH siss) An abnormal curving of the spine to the side.

trial (TRYE uhl) The act of trying or testing something; a test.

Research, Interviews, and Special Thanks _____

Additional research conducted at:
- Special Collections, Dartmouth College Library, Hanover, New Hampshire
- Milne Special Collections, University of New Hampshire Library, Durham, NH
- William Morris Hunt Memorial Library of the Museum of Fine Arts in Boston

Interviews held with:
- May Sidore Gruber
- Doris "Granny D." Rollins Haddock
- Former Governor Jeanne Shaheen
- Penny Pitou
- Charles "Chuck" Thorndike

Special thanks to:
- James Archer Abbott, Curator Woodrow Wilson House, Washington, D.C.
- Rebecca Courser, Executive Director of the Warner Historical Society's Executive Board
- Donald V. Fadely, author of *Hair-Raising Stories*
- Vicki E.D. Flanders, Historical Society of Cheshire County
- Dave Gaudes, Bernice Blake Perry's nephew
- Laura Kiernan, Judicial Branch Communications Director, NH Supreme Court
- Lesli Larson, Photographic Services, University of Oregon Libraries
- Nancy Mason, the Milne Collection at the UNH Library
- Barbara Miles, aviatrix and historian
- Ruth Nyblod, United States Patent Office
- Teresa Steer, Photo Archivist at the MacDowell Colony
- C. Wilson Sullivan, attorney to Bernice Blake Perry
- Carolyn Tremblay, Research Librarian at the Dover Public Library

A complete research bibliography for *Women of Granite: 25 New Hampshire Women You Should Know* is available in a downloadable PDF format from Apprentice Shop Books, LLC at www.apprenticeshopbooks.com

Partial Research Bibliography*

CHAPTER 1: Amias Thompson: *Settler*

Adams, James T. The Founding of New England. New York, NY: Atlantic Monthly P, 1921. Classics of American History. 8 Jan. 2008 < http://www.dinsdoc.com/adams-1-5.htm > Chapter 5 "The First Permanent Settlements"

"Amias, Our Grandmother." THOM(P)SON Tidbits. 8 Jan. 2008 < http://www.wellswooster.com/tommies/amiasour.htm >

Brewster, Edith Gilman. Some Three Hundred Years Ago. Concord, NH: The W. B. Ranney Company, 1922.

Daniell, Jere R. Colonial New Hampshire a History. Millwood, N.Y.: KTO P, 1981.

Fraser, Genevieve C. DAVID THOMSON, THE SCOTTISH FOUNDER OF NEW HAMPSHIRE. 1998. 8 Jan. 2008 < http://www.scotsgenealogy.com/onlineinformation.htm >

Robinson, J. Dennis. "David Thomson Vs the Pilgrims." SeacoastNH.Com (2005). 13 Jan. 2008 < http://seacoastnh.com/History/As_I_Please/David_Thomson_Vs_the_Pilgrims/ >

Robinson, J. Dennis. "Turkeygate: the Thanksgiving Scandal." SeacoastNH.Com (1996). < http://seacoastnh.com/Today/Editor_at_Large/Turkeygate%2C_The_Thanksgiving_Scandal/ >

Ward, Flora Lusk. David Thomson. Ms. < http://www.hodgman.org/thomson/ward-thomson.pdf. > 1947.

CHAPTER 2: Ona (Oney) Maria Judge Staines: *A Thirst for Freedom*

Hirschfeld, Fritz. George Washington and Slavery: a Documentary Portrayal. Columbia, MO: University of Missouri P, 1997.

Lawler, Edward, Jr. "Oney Judge." The President's House in Philadelphia. Independence Hall Association. 12 Jan. 2008 < http://www.ushistory.org/presidentshouse/slaves/oney.htm >

"Ona Maria Judge." Weeks Public Library. 02 Nov. 2005. 12 Jan. 2008 < http://www.weekslibrary.org/ona_maria_judge.htm > .

Sammons, Mark J., and Valerie Cunningham. Black Portsmouth: Three Centuries of African-American Heritage. Hanover, NH: University P of New England, 2004.

CHAPTER 3: Lucy Howe Crawford: *Innkeeper*

Burt, F. Allen. The Story of Mount Washington. 1st ed. Hanover, NH: Dartmouth Publications, 1960. 10-51.

Crawford, Lucy. History of the White Mountains. Ed. Stearns Morse. Hanover, NH: Dartmouth College, 1966.

Fabyan, Horace. Mount Washington House. New York, NY: Baker, Godwin and Co., 1852.

"History of Crawford Notch State Park." State of New Hampshire Division of Parks and Recreation. 4 Aug. 2007 < http://www.nhparks.state.nh.us/ParksPages/CrawfordNotch/CrawfordNotch.html >

Mudge, John T. B. The White Mountains Names, Places & Legends. 1st Ed. Etna, N.H: Durand P, 1992.

CHAPTER 4: Betsey Chamberlain: *A Chance to Write*

Gravel, Diane F., and David W. Kruger, eds. New Hampshire Families in 1790. Special Publication No. 10. Vol. I. Concord, NH: New Hampshire Society of Genealogists, 2007.

Packer, Joy, and Kenneth M. Roemer, eds. The Cambridge Companion to Native American Literature. New York: Cambridge UP, 2005.

Ranta, Judith A. The Life and Writings of Betsey Chamberlain: Native American Mill Worker. Boston: Northeastern UP, 2003.

CHAPTER 5: Harriet E.A. Wilson: *African-American Novelist*

A Black History Tour: Milford, Harriet Wilson and the Anti-Slavery Movement. Milford, NH: The Harriet Wilson Project, 2005 < www.harrietwilsonproject.org >

Boggis, Jerrianne, Eve Allegra Raimon, and Barbara A. White, eds. Harriet Wilson's New England: Race, Writing and Region. Durham, NH: University of New Hampshire, 2007.

Gewertz, Ken. "First African-American Woman Novelist Revisited." Harvard Gazette (2005). 11 Oct. 2007 < http://www.news.harvard.edu/gazette/2005/03.24/09-wilson.html > .

Wilson, Harriet E., P. Gabrielle Foreman, and Reginald H. Pitts. Our Nig, or, Sketches From the Life of a Free Black. New York: Penguin Books, 2005.

CHAPTER 6: Margaret "Mattie" Knight: *Distinguished Bag Lady*

"Hall of Fame/Inventor Profile." Invent.Org. < http://www.invent.org/Hall_Of_Fame/285.html > .

"Margaret E. Knight." Paper Industry International Hall of Fame. < http://www.paperhall.org/inductees/bios/2006/margaret_knight.php > .

Women Who are Inventors." The New York Times 19 Oct. 1913. The New York Times. 24 Jan. 2008.

CHAPTER 7: Marilla Ricker: *Suffragette*

"Freethought of the Day Marilla M. Ricker." Freedom From Religion Foundation. 18 Mar. 2007. 23 July 2007 http://ffrf.org/day/?day=18&month=3

Gray, Carole. "Children of Free Thought." The American Atheist 37 (1998). 23 July 2007 http://www.americanatheist.org/win98-99/T1/gray.html

Makem, Connor. "Women's Equality Day: Remembering Marilla Ricker." Rochester Times. 23 July 2007 < http://www.maineaflcio.org.women%20history%20equality%20day%20marilla%20ricker&type >

Richey, Leeann. Reading Between the Lines: Marilla Ricker in the Struggle for Women's Rights. Diss. Stanford Univ. 11 Aug. 2007 < http://womenslegalhistory.stanford.edu/papers/Marillapapers.pdf >

continued Partial Research Bibliography*

CHAPTER 8: Marian MacDowell: *An Ordinary Woman*

Brown, Janice. "Peterborough, New Hampshire Art Patron and Pianist: Marian Griswold (Nevins) MacDowell (1857-1956)."

Guides to Special Collections in the Music Division of the Library of Congress: Edward and Marian MacDowell Collection. Vers. Biographical Notes. Library of Congress. 01 Sept. 2007 < http://lcweb2loc.gov/service/music/eadxmlmusic/mu2005.wp.0024.pdf >

"MacDowell Colony." Time 31 Jan. 1938. 09 Sept. 2007 http://www.time.com/time/magazine/article/0,9171,759089.00.html

Rausch, Robin, comp. The House That Marian Built: the MacDowell Colony of Peterborough, New Hampshire. Vers. Online Version. 2001. Library of Congress. 01 Sept. 2007 < http://memory.loc.gov/ammem/awhhtnl/aw08e/aw08e.html >.

"The MacDowell Colony." The MacDowell Colony. 03 Sept. 2007 < http://www.macdowellcolony.org >.

CHAPTER 9: Mary Bradish Titcomb: *She Worked Hard at her Craft*

Annual Reports of the Town of Windham, New Hampshire, 1863-1928. Cities vary: Town of Windham, NH.

Jarzombek, Nancy Allyn. Mary Bradish Titcomb and Her Contemporaries: the Artists of the Fenway Studios 1905-1939: May 30-July 31, 1998. Boston: Vose Galleries, 1998.

Waitt, Marian P. "President Buys of Boston Artist: Miss Titcomb's Portrait of 'Geraldine J.' is in White House." Boston Journal 6 Feb. 1915: 5.

CHAPTER 10: Caroline Gardner Clark Bartlett: *Nurse or Spy?*

"'Sister Beatrice' Accused." The New York Times 4 Dec. 1915: 7.

"Boston Singer Tells of War Nurses' Experiences." The Portsmouth Herald 24 Aug. 1915: 4. NewspaperARCHIVE.Com.

Davis, Connie. "An Angel of Mercy Accused of Spying." The Chronicle-Telegram 4 June 2002, sec. B: 6. NewspaperARCHIVE.Com.

"False Charge Made Against Mrs. Caroline G. Gardner." The Elyria Chronicle 4 Dec. 1915: 1. NewspaperARCHIVE.Com.

"Recognized for Work During World War." The Chronicle-Telegram 14 June 1929: 1-2. NewspaperARCHIVE.Com.

"Singer is War Nurse." The Washington Post 5 Sept. 1915: 11. NewspaperARCHIVE.Com.

"Sister Beatrice Pleads for Supplies for French Hospitals." Elyria Evening Telegram 12 Nov. 1915: 1. NewspaperARCHIVE.Com.

CHAPTER 11: Persis Foster Eames Albee: *Business Pioneer*

"1920 United States Federal Census." Ancestry.Com. 18 Jan. 2008 < http://search.ancestry.com/cgibin/sse.dll?rank = 0&gsfn = Ellery&gsln = Albee&sx = &f8 = New + York&f9 = Westchester&f10 = dobbs + ferry&f20 = New + Hampshire&rg_fa5__date = 1832&rs_fa5__date = 0&f16__n = &rg_f19__date = &rs_f19__date = 0&f18 = &fa20 = &f21 = &fa18 = &f22 = &fa14 = &gskw = &prox = 1&db = 1920usfedcen&ti = 0&ti.si = 0&gl = &gss = IMAGE&gst = &so = 3 >

Flanders, Vicki E. "Persis Foster Eames Albee: the First 'Avon Lady'" Historical Society of Cheshire County, New Hampshire. 2007. < http://www.hsccnh.org/educationhp/hp8.cfm > .

Klepacki, Laura. Avon: Building the World's Premier Company for Women. Hoboken, NJ: John Wiley & Sons, 2005.

"Years of Shamming." The Sunday Gazette: Fort Wayne, Ind. 31 Jan. 1886: 7. NewspaperARCHIVE.Com.

CHAPTER 12: Elizabeth Gurley Flynn: *Fighting Injustice*

Baxandall, Rosalyn F. Words on Fire: the Life and Writing of Elizabeth Gurley Flynn. New Brunswick, NJ: Rutgers UP, 1987.

Camp, Helen C. Iron in Her Soul: Elizabeth Gurley Flynn and the American Left. Pullman, WA: WSU P, 1995.

Flynn, Elizabeth G. I Speak My Own Piece: Autobiography of "the Rebel Girl" New York: Masses & Mainstream, 1955.

Flynn, Elizabeth G. The Alderson Story: My Life as a Political Prisoner. New York: International, 1963.

Flynn, Elizabeth G. The Rebel Girl: an Autobiography: My First Life (1906-1926). New, Revised ed. New York: International, 1973.

CHAPTER 13: Lotte Jacobi: *Photographic Artist*

"Artists: Lotte Jacobi." The Getty. The Getty Museum. 4 Aug. 2007 < http://www.getty.edu/art/gettyguide/artMakerDetails?maker = 1788 > .

"Arts & Artists: Lotte Jacobi." NH State Council on the Arts. 2004. State of New Hampshire. 20 Aug. 2007 < http:www.nh.gov/nharts/artsandartists/inmemory/lottejacobi.html > .

Fasanelli, James A. "Lotte Jacobi: Photographer." Introduction. Lotte Jacobi. By Kelly Wise (Ed.). Danbury, NH: Addison House, 1978.

Jacobi, Lotte. Notes Written by Lotte Jacobi. Ms. Box 32, F12. University of New Hampshire, Milne Special Collections, New Hampshire.

Shouldis, Victoria. "A Life in Black and White." Concord Monitor 13 Nov. 2003, sec. D: 01. Concord Monitor Online. Newsbank. 22 Aug. 2007.

Wise, Kelly, ed. Lotte Jacobi. Danbury, NH: Addison House, 1978.

* A complete research bibliography is available in downloadable PDF format from www.apprenticeshopbooks.com

continued Partial Research Bibliography*

CHAPTER 14: Bernice Blake Perry: NH's *Queen of the Air*

"Bernice Blake Perry Scrapbooks." Multiple Sources.

Gaudes, David. Telephone interview. 14 Oct. 2007.

CHAPTER 15: Elizabeth Yates: *Newbery Award Winning Author*

"Elizabeth Yates: Bringing History to Life." Authors and Books for Children. 27 Sept. 2007 < http://www.elliemik. com/yates.html > .

Graham, Jim. "Renowned Author Yates Dies At 95." The Concord Monitor 1 Aug. 2001. 4 Oct. 2007 < http:// cache.zoominfo.com/CachedPage/?archive_id = 0&page_ id = 180256250 > .

Hendryx, Nancy. "Kindred Spirits." Concord Monitor 20 Oct. 1999. 4 Oct. 2007.

Trudell P.m., Sister Margaret. Elizabeth Yates: a Biography and Bibliography of Her Works. 1st Books Library, 2003.

Yates, Elizabeth. Spanning Time: a Diary Keeper Becomes a Writer. Peterborough, NH: Cobblestone, Inc., 1996.

Chapter 16: Elizabeth Orton Jones: *Old Girl, You Are an Artist!*

Carey, Alice. "Twig's Vision." The Horn Book Magazine Sept. 2005.

Helmer, N. "Twentieth-Century American Children's Literature - Elizabeth Orton Jones." UO Libraries. 23 Apr. 2004. University of Oregon. < http://libweb.uoregon. edu/ec/exhibits/childrenslit/eojones.html > .

Jones, Elizabeth O. "Horn Book Reminiscences From Elizabeth Orton Jones." The Horn Book, Inc. Sept.-Oct. 1999. < http://www.hbook.com/magazine/articles/1999/ sep99_jones.asp > .

Salisbury, Jessie. "A Twig with Strong Roots." Nashua Sunday Telegraph 30 Dec. 2001. < http://www.purplehousepress. com/nashua.htm > .

CHAPTER 17: Doris "Granny D" Haddock: *Fighting for a Better America*

"Granny D Rocks the Vote, on Tour." National Public Radio. 14 Mar. 2004. 09 Oct. 2007 < http://www.npr.org/ templates/story/story.php?storyId = 1690738 > .

Haddock, Doris, and Dennis M. Burke. Granny D: Walking Across America in My 90th Year. New York: Villard Books, a Division of Random House, 2001.

Haddock, Granny D. "Senators, How Did You Dare Think We Do Not Care?" 29 Feb. 2000. Speech Given on Steps of US Capitol. 07 Oct. 2007 < http://www.awakenedwoman. com/GrannyD.htm > .

Run, Granny, Run. Documentary. Director: Marlo Poras. Performer: E. Doris "Granny D" Haddock. DVD. 2007.

CHAPTER 18: May Sidore Gruber: *Knitting the Pandora Empire*

Gruber, May. Pandora's Pride. New York: Lyle Stuart, Inc., 1985.

Gruber, May. Personal interview. 15 Oct. 2007.

Gruber, May. Sky Hooks and Track Shoes. Amherst, New Hampshire: Brick House Company, 1989.

CHAPTER 19: Annalee Thorndike: *Doll Maker and Businesswoman*

Annalee: The Story Behind the Dolls. Meredith, NH: Annalee Mobilitee Dolls, Inc. Company pamphlet.

Brown, Janice. "Meredith New Hampshire Doll Maker Barbara Annalee (Davis) Thorndike (1915-2002)." Cow Hampshire: Blogging About New Hampshire History, Genealogy, Photography and Humor. 21 June 2006. < http://cowhampshire.blogharbor.com/blog/_archives/20 06/6/21/2022724.html > .

"Museum of New Hampshire History: the Dolls of Annalee." New Hampshire Historical Society. 20 Dec. 2007. 6 May 2007 < http://www.nhhistory.org/annaleeexhibit.html > .

"The Story of Annalee." Annalee. Annalee Mobilitee Dolls, Inc. < http://www.annalee.com/ourstory.asp > .

"The Story of a Young Girl Named Barbara Annalee Thorndike." Annalee. Annalee Mobilitee Dolls. < http:// www.annalee.com/annaleetimeline.asp > .

CHAPTER 20: Penny Pitou: *She Keeps Going and Going and...*

Merron, Jeff, and Eric Neel. "1960 Squaw Valley." ESPN Sports. 18 Dec. 2001. 10 Sept. 2007 < http://sports.espn. go.com./oly/winter02/gen/feature?page = history1960 > .

"Penny Pitou Established Permanent Fund." New Hampshire Charitable Foundation. 09 Sept. 2007 < http://www.nhcf. org/newsarticle.cfm?articleid = 5460&ptsidebarptid > .

"Penny Pitou." Newhampshire.Com. 09 Sept. 2007 < http:// www.newhampshire.com/nh-people/penny-pitou- biography.aspx > .

Penny Pitou: phone interview, Friday, October 12, 2007.

"Sportsline." CBS Sports. 10 Sept. 2007 < http://www. sportsline.com/olympics/winter/history/1960 > .

Sullivan, Joe. "Skier Pitou Inducted Into New England Hall of Fame." Manchester Union Leader 05 Nov. 2001.

"Trial by Snow." Time 07 Mar. 1960. 10 Sept. 2007 < http:// www.time.com/time/magazine/article/0,9171,939131,00. html > .

Chapter 21: Jeanne Shaheen: *NH's First Elected Woman Governor*

Doris, Margaret. "The Political Machine." Boston.Com. < http://www.boston.com/news/globe/magazine/ articles/2005/11/06/the_political_machine/ >

Jeanne Shaheen. < jeanneshaheen.org >.

Shaheen, Jeanne. Telephone interview. 23 Nov. 2007.

CHAPTER 22: Christa McAuliffe: *Teacher in Space*

"Biographical Data, S. Christa Corrigan McAuliffe Teacher in Space Participant (deceased)." Lyndon B. Johnson Space Center. National Aeronautics and Space Administration. 11 June 2007 < http://www.jsc.nasa.gov/Bios/htmlbios/mcauliffe.html >.

Burgess, Colin. Teacher in Space: Christa McAuliffe and the Challenger Legacy. Lincoln: University of Nebraska Press, 2000.

"Christa McAuliffe (1948-1986)." Framingham.Com. 11 June 2007 < http://www.framingham.com/history/profiles/christa.htm >.

"Christa McAuliffe: a Biography." Christa McAuliffe Planetarium. 8 May 2007 < http://www.starhop.com/cm_bio.htm >.

"The Shuttle Explosion, the Seven Who Perished in the Explosion of the Challenger." The New York Times on the Web 29 Jan. 1986. < http://www.nytimes.com/learning/general/onthisday/bday/0902.html >.

CHAPTER 23: Linda Stewart Dalianis: *NH's First Woman Supreme Court Justice*

"About the Superior Court." New Hampshire Superior Court. 25 July 2007 < http://www.courts.state.nh.us/superior/about.htm >.

Dalianis, Linda S. "NH Bar Journal Issue Re: NH Judiciary and Vologda, Russia Courts." New Hampshire Bar Association. 15 May 2007 < http://www.nhbar.org/publications/archives/display-journal-issue.asp?id = 106 >.

Landrigan, Kevin. "Dalianis Makes History: Nashuan is First Woman Sworn in to State Supreme Court." Nashua Telegraph 27 Apr. 2000. Telegraph Publishing Company News and Obituaries Archive. Newsbank. 15 May 2007.

"National News Briefs: New Hampshire Names Woman for Top Court." The New York Times 27 Apr. 2000. Nytimes.Com. 10 May 2007.

"Shaheen Gets to Appoint Judge to All-Male Court." New Hampshire Union Leader 31 Aug. 1999. Newsbank. 16 May 2007

"Supreme Court:: Senior Associate Justice Linda S. Dalianis." Judicial Branch, State of New Hampshire. 7 May 2007 < http://www.courts.state.nh.us/supreme/meetdalian.htm >.

Wolfe, Andrew. "Dalianis Wears Robe of Pioneer in Legal Field with Humor, Aplomb." Nashua Telegraph 27 Apr. 2000. Telegraph Publishing Company News and Obituaries Archive. Newsbank. 15 May 2007.

CHAPTER 24: Lynn Jennings: *Distance Runner*

""American Female Runner of 1993: Lynn Jennings"" Runner World 1994: 88. MasterFILE Premier. EBSCO Publishing. Bedford Public Library. 11 May 2007.

"Balancing Act." Runner World 1996: 70. MasterFILE Premier. EBSCO. Bedford Public Library. 11 May 2007.

"Head Coach: John Babington." Wellsley Cross Country. 19 Apr. 2007. Wellsley College. 30 May 2007 < http://www.wellesley.edu/Athletics/Crosscountry/coach.html >.

Litsky, Frank. "Lynn Jennings Makes Retirement Official." The New York Times 23 Mar. 2006. Nytimes.Com. 17 May 2007.

"Lynn Jennings." National Distance Running Hall of Fame. 2005. 17 May 2007 < http://www.distancrunning.com/inductees/2001/jennings.html >.

"Spotlight: Lynn Jennings." Sports Illustrated Women. 9 Apr. 1999. 17 May 2007 < http://sportsillustrated.cnn.com/siforwomen/news/1999/04/09/spotlight >.

"USATF Athlete Biography: Lynn Jennings." United States Track and Field. 11 May 2007 < http://www.usatf.org/athletes/bios/oldBios/2000/jenningsl.html >.

"USTAF Hall of Fame Class of 2006 Interviews." Running Times Magazine. 24 Nov. 2006. 30 May 2007 < http://www.runningtimesmagazine.com/rt/articles/?c = 74&id-9490 >.

CHAPTER 25: Jenny Thompson: *Olympic Swimmer*

"Athlete Bio: Jenny Thompson." Usolympicteam.Com, the Official Site of the US Olympic Team. 2004. United States Olympic Committee. < http://www.usoc.org/26_1247.htm >.

Eymer, Rick. "Thompson Tops Hall of Fame Inductees." Palo Alto Online 6 Sept. 2007. 22 Sept. 2007 < http://www.paloaltoonline.com/news/show_story.php?id = 5760 >.

"New Hampshire People: Jenny Thompson." Newhampsire.Com, New Hampshire's Homepage. 2008. The Union Leader Corporation. < http://www.newhampshire.com/nh-people/jenny-thompson-biography.aspx >.

Scott, Paula P. "Jenny Thompson Biography- Chronology, Awards and Accomplishments, Further Information - CONTACT INFORMATION." Famous Sports Stars. 2008. Net Industries. < http://sports.jrank.org/pages/4827/Thompson-Jenny.html >.

"Swim Heroes: Jenny Thompson." Swim City. 2007. < http://swim-city.com/swimheroes.php3?hero = jenny_thompson >.

"USA Swimming: Jenny Thompson." USA Swimming Official Website. 2004. < http://www.usaswimming.org/USASWeb/DesktopModules/BioViewManaged.aspx?personid = 5560a9e4-7ba0-4049-ad2e-0184b42f86bd&TabId = 388&Mid = 597 >.

* A complete research bibliography is available in downloadable PDF format from www.apprenticeshopbooks.com